CALLAN
METHOD

# Student's Book
## Stage 5

**English in a quarter of the time!**

The Callan ® Method was first developed and published
in 1960 by R.K. T. Callan.
This edition was published for the international market in 2012.



**Student's Book – Stage 5**
ISBN 978-1-908954-16-9



Printed in the EU

**Conditions of sale**



**Published by**

CALLAN PUBLISHING LTD.
Orchard House, 45-47 Mill Way, Grantchester, Cambridge CB3 9ND
in association with CALLAN METHOD ORGANISATION LTD.

www.callan.co.uk

CALLAN
METHOD

- Para obtener la traducción de este prefacio en español, visitar
  www.callan.co.uk/preface/es
- Per una traduzione di questa prefazione in Italiano, visitare il sito
  www.callan.co.uk/preface/it
- Para obter uma tradução deste prefácio em português, visite
  www.callan.co.uk/preface/pt
- Z polskim tłumaczeniem tego wstępu można zapoznać się na stronie
  www.callan.co.uk/preface/pl
- Pour obtenir la traduction de cette préface en français, rendez-vous sur le site
  www.callan.co.uk/preface/fr
- Bu önsözün Türkçe çevirisi için aşağıdaki web adresini ziyaret edin
  www.callan.co.uk/preface/tr
- 本序言的中文翻译，请访问
  www.callan.co.uk/preface/ch
- 前書きの日本語版の翻訳は次ページをご覧ください
  www.callan.co.uk/preface/jp
- للاطلاع على ترجمة هذه المقدمة باللغة العربية يرجى زيارة
  www.callan.co.uk/preface/ar

# Welcome to the Callan Method

## Learning English with the Callan™ Method is fast and effective!

The Callan Method is a teaching method created specifically to improve your English in an intensive atmosphere. The teacher is constantly asking questions, so you are hearing and using the language as much as possible. When you speak in the lesson, the teacher corrects your grammar and pronunciation mistakes, and you learn a lot from this correction.

The Callan Method teaches English vocabulary and grammar in a carefully programmed way, with systematic revision and reinforcement. In the lesson, there is a lot of speaking and listening practice, but there is also reading and writing so that you revise and consolidate what you have learned.

With the Callan Method, the teacher speaks quickly so that you learn to understand English when it is spoken at natural speed. This also means that everyone is concentrating hard all the time.

## English in a quarter of the time

The Callan Method can teach English in a quarter of the time taken by any other method on the market. Instead of the usual 350 hours necessary to get the average student to the level of the Cambridge Preliminary English Test (PET), the Callan Method can take as little as 80 hours, and only 160 hours for the Cambridge First Certificate in English (FCE).

The method is suitable for students of all nationalities, and ages. It requires no equipment (not even a whiteboard) or other books, and can be used for classes at private schools, state schools and universities. It is also possible for students to use the books to practise with each other when they are not at school.

In addition to this, students can practise their English online using the interactive exercises, which are available to students who study at licensed schools. Ask your school for details.

## The Callan Method in practice

A Callan Method English lesson is probably very different from lessons you have done in the past. You do not sit in silence, doing a reading comprehension test or a grammar exercise from a book. You do not have 'free conversation', where you only use the English you already feel comfortable with. Of course, activities like this can help you, but you can do them at home with a book, or in a coffee bar. In a Callan Method lesson, you are busy with important activities that you cannot do outside the classroom. You are listening to English all the time. You are speaking English a lot, and all your mistakes are corrected. You learn quickly because you are always surrounded by English. There is no silence and no time to get bored or lose your concentration. And it is also fun!

So, what exactly happens in a Callan Method lesson, and how does it work?

## The teacher asks you questions

The Callan Method books are full of questions. Each question practises a word, an expression, or a piece of grammar. The teacher is standing, and asks the questions to the students one by one. You never know when the teacher will ask you, so you are always concentrating. When one student finishes answering one question, the teacher immediately starts to ask the next question.

## The teacher speaks quickly

The teacher in a Callan Method lesson speaks quickly. This is because, in the real world, it is natural to speak quickly. If you want to understand normal English, you must practise listening to quick natural speech and become able to understand English without first translating into your language. This idea of not translating is at the centre of the Callan Method; this method helps you to start thinking in English.

Also, we do not want you to stop and think a lot about the grammar while you are speaking. We want you to speak as a reflex, instinctively. And do not worry about mistakes. You will, naturally, make a lot of mistakes in the lessons, but Callan Method teachers correct your mistakes, and you learn from the corrections. When you go home, of course it will help if you read your book, think about the grammar, study the vocabulary, and do all the things that language students do at home – but the lessons are times to practise your listening and speaking, with your books closed!

## The teacher says every question twice, and helps you with the answer

In the lesson, the teacher speaks quickly, so we say the questions twice. This way, you have another chance to listen if you did not understand everything the first time.

The teacher then immediately says the beginning of the answer. This is to help you (and 'push' you) to start speaking immediately. So, for example:

**Teacher:** *"Are there two chairs in this room? Are there two chairs in this room? No, there aren't ..."*

**Student** (immediately): *"No, there aren't two chairs in this room; there are twelve chairs in this room."*

If the teacher does not 'push' you by giving you the beginning of the answer, you might start to think too much, and translate into your language.

The teacher will speak along with you all the time while you are saying your answer. So, if you forget a word or you are not sure what to say, you will always hear the next word or two from the teacher. You should repeat after the teacher, but immediately try again to continue with the answer yourself. You must always try to continue speaking, and only copy the teacher when you cannot continue alone. That way, you will become more confident and learn more quickly. Never simply wait for help from the teacher and then copy – you will not improve so quickly.

## Long answers, with the same grammar as the question

We want you to practise your speaking as much as possible, so you always make complete sentences when you speak in the lesson, using the same grammatical structure as in the question. For example:

**Teacher:** *"About how many pages are there in this book?"*

**Student:** *"There are about two hundred pages in that book."*

In this way, you are not just answering a question; you are making full sentences with the vocabulary and the grammar that you need to learn.

## Correction by imitation

With the Callan Method, the teacher corrects all your mistakes the moment you make them. The teacher corrects you by imitating (copying) your mistake and then saying the correct pronunciation/form of the word. For example, if you say "He come from Spain", the teacher quickly says "not come - ***comes***". This correction by imitation helps you to hear the difference between your mistake and the proper English form. You should immediately repeat the correct word and continue with your sentence. You learn a lot from this correction of your mistakes, and constant correction results in fast progress.

## Contracted forms

In the lesson, the teacher uses contractions (e.g. the teacher says "I don't" instead of "I do not"). This is because it is natural to use contractions in spoken English and you must learn to understand them. Also, if you want to sound natural when you speak, you must learn to use contractions.

## Lesson structure

Every school is different, but a typical 50-minute Callan lesson will contain about 35 minutes of speaking, a 10-minute period for reading, and a 5-minute dictation. The reading practice and the dictation are often in the middle of the lesson.

In the reading part, you read and speak while the teacher helps you and corrects your mistakes. In the dictation, you practise your writing, but you are also listening to the teacher. So, a 50-minute Callan lesson is 50 minutes of spoken English with no silence!

## No chatting

Although the Callan Method emphasises the importance of speaking practice, this does not mean chatting (free conversation). You learn English quickly with the Callan Method partly because the lessons are organised, efficient, fast and busy. There is no time wasted on chatting; this can be done before or after the lesson.

Chatting is not a good way to spend your time in an English lesson. First, only some of the students speak. Second, in a chat, people only use the English that they already know. Third, it is difficult for a teacher to correct mistakes during a conversation.

The Callan Method has none of these problems. All through the lesson, every student is listening and speaking, practising different vocabulary and structures, and learning from the correction of their mistakes. And nobody has time to get bored!

# Repeat, repeat, repeat!

## Systematic revision

In your native language, you sometimes read or hear a word that you do not already know. You usually need to read or hear this new word only once or twice in order to remember it and then use it yourself. However, when you are learning a foreign language, things are very different. You need to hear, see and use words and grammatical structures many times before you really know them properly. So your studies must involve a system of revision (repeating what you have studied before). This is absolutely essential. If there is no system of revision in your studies, you will forget what you have studied and will not be able to speak or understand better than before.

In every Callan Method lesson, of course you learn new English, practise it, and progress through your book. However, you also do a lot of revision so that you can really learn what you have studied. Your teacher can decide how much revision your class needs, but it will always be an important part of your studies.

Also, because there is a lot of revision, it is not important for you to understand everything the first time; it gets easier. The revision with Callan is automatic and systematic. Every day you do a lot of revision and then learn some new English.

## Revision in reading and dictation too

The reading and dictation practice in the lessons is part of Callan's systematic revision as well. First, you learn a new word in the speaking part of the lesson; a few lessons later, you meet it again when you are reading; finally, the word appears in a dictation. This is all written into the Callan Method; it happens automatically.

## Correcting your dictations

With the Callan Method, there is little or no homework to do, but it is very important that you correct your dictations. These are printed in your book and so you can easily correct them at home, on the bus, or wherever. It is important to do this because it helps you to learn the written forms of the words you have already studied in earlier lessons.

## Your first lessons with the Callan Method

During your first lesson with the Callan Method, all of the questions and some of the vocabulary are new for you; you have not done any revision yet. For this reason, the teacher may not ask you many questions. You can sit and listen, and become more familiar with the method - the speed, the questions, the correction etc.

## History of the Callan Method – Robin Callan

Robin Callan is the creator of the Callan Method. He owns the Callan School in London's Oxford Street. He also runs Callan Publishing Limited, which supplies Callan Method books to schools all over the world.

Robin Callan grew up in Ely, Cambridgeshire, England. In his early twenties, he went to Italy to teach English in Salerno. Although he enjoyed teaching, Robin thought that the way in which teachers were expected to teach their lessons was inefficient and boring. He became very interested in the mechanisms of language learning, and was sure that he could radically improve the way English was taught.

He remained in Italy and started to write his own books for teaching English. He used these in his own classes and, over the following ten years, gained an immense amount of practical experience and a reputation for teaching English quickly and effectively.

When he returned to England, he opened his school in Oxford Street. As the method became more and more popular with students, the school grew and moved to larger premises. Robin continued to write his Callan Method books, and today the method is used by schools all over the world.

Robin Callan has always been passionate about English literature, especially poetry. For this reason, he bought The Orchard Tea Garden in Grantchester, near Cambridge, which attracts thousands of tourists each year. Throughout the 20th century, it was a popular meeting place for many famous Cambridge University students and important figures from English literature, such as Rupert Brooke, Virginia Woolf and E.M. Forster. Today, it is also home to the Rupert Brooke Museum.

Mr Callan now lives in Grantchester, but still plays an active role in the management of the Callan School in London.

# The Callan School in London's Oxford Street

## The largest private school in London

The Callan School in Oxford Street is the largest private school in London teaching English as a foreign language. Depending on the time of year, the school employs between 60 and 100 teachers and has an average of 1600 students passing through its doors every day. This number rises to more than 2000 in the middle of summer, similar to a small university.

## Websites

Please visit the following websites for more information:

**Callan Method** http://www.callan.co.uk

Lots of information, including a list of schools around the world that use the method

**Callan School London** http://www.callanschoollondon.com/en/callan-school

All you need to know about the largest private English language school in London

## How Callan Method Stages compare to CEFR* levels and University of Cambridge General English exams

** Common European Framework of Reference*

It is difficult to compare the Callan Method books directly with the CEFR levels and Cambridge exams, but below is an approximate guide.

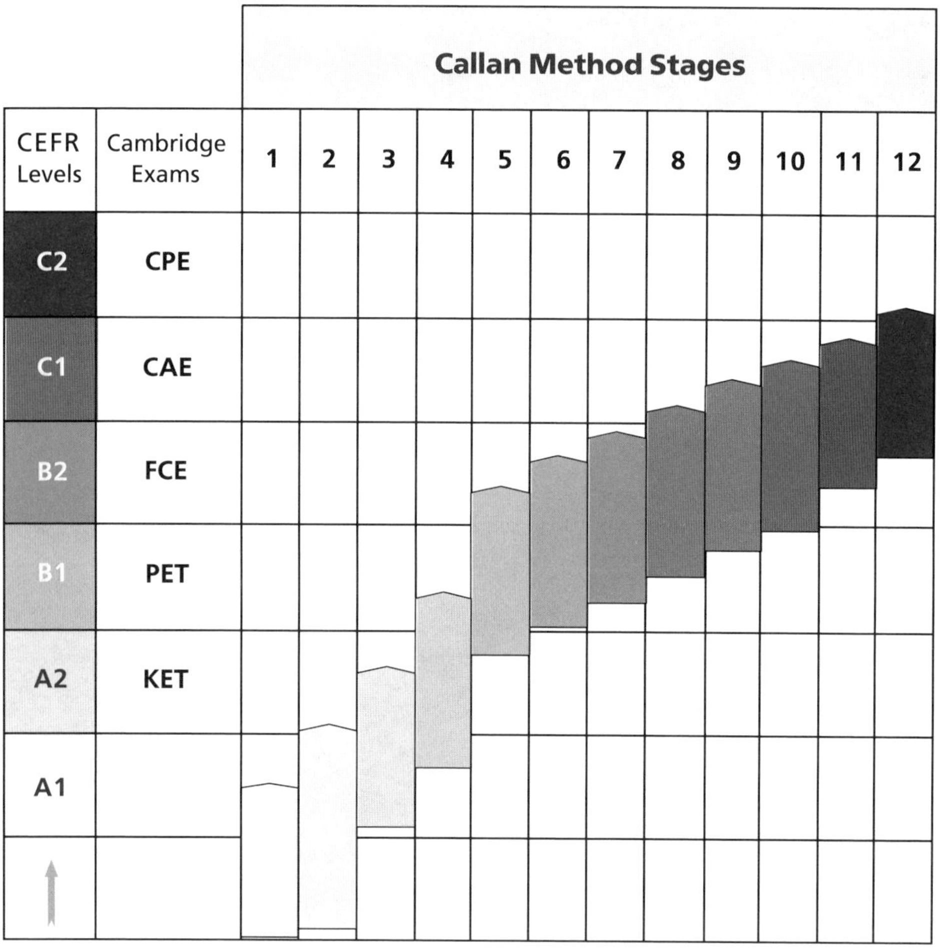

# STAGE 5

# LESSON 61

315 **chat** **online**

Do you prefer chatting with your friends on the phone or online?
I prefer chatting with my friends ...

Why?

How often do you go online to look at your email?
I go online ... to look at my email

**notice**

Do you notice anything different about the classroom today?
Yes, I notice something different ... ~ No, I don't notice anything different ...

What's the first thing you notice about people when you meet them for the first time?
The first thing I notice about people when I meet them for the first time is their voice (clothes, eyes etc.)

**free** **busy**

Are most people busy on Sunday?
No, most people aren't ...; they're free

What do we mean by a free meal?
By a free meal, we mean that we don't have to pay for it

Do you believe that the best things in life are free?
Yes, I believe ... ~ No, I don't believe ...

316 **lie** **comfortable** **uncomfortable**

**pillow**

Is the book standing on the table?
No, the book isn't standing ...; it's lying ...

Is it more comfortable to sleep lying down or sitting up? It's more comfortable to sleep lying down than sitting up

Do you find it comfortable to sleep without a pillow? Yes, I find it ... ~ No, I don't find it ...; I find it uncomfortable

**wake up – woke up – woken up**

**go to sleep** **immediately** **midnight**

Do you usually go to sleep before midnight? Yes, I usually ... ~ No, I don't usually ...

Do you generally wake up early? Yes, I generally ... ~ No, I don't generally ...

What are the three forms of "wake up"? The three forms of "wake up" are "wake up, woke up, woken up"

What was the first thing you saw when you woke up today? The first thing I saw when I woke up ...

Have you ever woken up too late to go to school (or work)? Yes, I've sometimes woken up ... ~ No, I've never woken up ...

317 **through** **button** **buttonhole**

What am I doing? You're putting your pen through the buttonhole in your shirt (blouse etc.)

When you look through your bedroom window, what do you see? When I look through my bedroom window, I see ...

If you went from London to Rome, which cities would you perhaps have to go through? If I went ..., I would perhaps have to go through Paris, Milan etc.

**career**

Would you like a career in the army? Yes, I'd like ... ~ No, I wouldn't like ...

**cross** **crossroads** **test**

What's this? It's a cross

When a teacher puts a cross next to an answer in a written test, what does it mean? When a teacher ..., it means the answer is wrong

Are there any crossroads at the end of the street where you live? Yes, there are some ... where I live ~ No, there aren't any ... where I live

318 **danger** **dangerous** **dangerously**

**alcohol** **detective**

What colour do we use for danger? We use red for danger

Is it dangerous to drive after drinking alcohol? Yes, it's dangerous ...

Would you like to live dangerously like a detective: somebody like Sherlock Holmes, for example? Yes, I'd like ... ~ No, I wouldn't like ...

**should** **obligation** **alternative**

**ambulance**

**The sentences "I must study" and "I should study" are not the same. The first sentence, "I must study", means that I have an obligation to study; I have no alternative. The second sentence, "I should study", means that I have alternatives; I can go to the cinema if I like, or for a walk, but studying is the right thing for me to do. The best idea is to study.**

What's the difference between these two sentences: "I must study" and "I should study"? The difference between those two sentences is that "I must study" means that I have no alternative, whereas "I should study" means I have alternatives but that studying is the right thing for me to do

How do we translate "I must study"? We translate "I must study" with ...

And how do we translate "I should study"? We translate "I should study" with ...

319 Do you think people should be more polite in the shops and streets? Yes, I think ...

Do you agree that students should study hard? Yes, I agree ...

Do you agree that young people should help the old? Yes, I agree ...

What should we do when somebody is dangerously ill? When somebody ..., we should immediately call an ambulance

What do you think you should do if you want to make a lot of money? If you want to ..., I think you should ...

**correct** **grammatical**

Do you correct your dictations during the lesson? Yes, I correct my dictations ... ~ No, I don't correct my dictations ...; I correct them after the lesson

In a Callan Method lesson, does the teacher correct your grammatical mistakes? Yes, in a Callan Method lesson, ...

How can we correct our mistakes in our pronunciation? We can correct ... by listening and speaking as much as possible

**problem** **cause** **colleague** **boss**

**freedom** **justice**

If you have a problem with a colleague at work, should you speak to your boss about it? Yes, if I have ..., I should speak to my boss about it

320 Can smoking cause health problems? Yes, smoking can ...

In history, have many people died for the causes of freedom and justice? Yes, in history, many people ...

**as**

As we have now studied about a thousand words and a lot of the grammar, can you hold a simple conversation in English? Yes, as we have ..., I can hold ...

As you are not tall enough to reach the ceiling, what would you have to do if you wanted to reach it? As I am not ..., I would have to put a chair on the table and stand on the chair if I wanted ...

## that is

**We use the words "that is" when we want to correct something we have just said, or when we want to add more information.**

Give me a sentence with "that is" in it.

Everybody loves that film; that is, everybody I've spoken to. We will go to the cinema this evening; that is, if we have enough money

## bone

Have you ever broken any of the bones in your body?

Yes, I've broken one/some of ... ~ No, I've never broken any of ...

When? How?

321 *Dictation 36*

If somebody wants/ to buy my motorbike/ before I go away,/ I'll sell it/ for almost nothing./ It is worth paying a little more,/ and going to a good hairdresser./ Parents often read/ bedtime stories to their children./ In some ways,/ life today is harder/ than it was in the past,/ but in other ways/ it is easier./ The waiter brought us the menu,/ but it was the waitress/ who brought the food.

# LESSON 62

322 **life** **lives** **the poor** **the rich**

**If a noun finishes with "f" or "fe", we make the plural by changing the "f" or "fe" to "ves". For example, the plural of "wife" is "wives"; the plural of "knife" is "knives"; the plural of "scarf" is "scarves".**

What's the plural of "life"? The plural of ...

Do you think the lives of the poor are happier than those of the rich? Yes, I think ... ~ No, I don't think ...; I think they're less happy

**although**

Make a sentence with the word "although" in it. Although the food was not very nice, I ate it because I was hungry

Although you're now able to hold a simple conversation in English, do you think you should keep studying? Yes, although I'm ..., I think I should ...

Are some people always happy although they have problems in their lives? Yes, some people ...

**cook** **tasty** **pasta**

Is there a restaurant near here that cooks tasty food? Yes, there's a ... ~ No, there isn't a ...

Is it difficult to cook pasta? No, it isn't difficult ...; it's easy

323 Are you a good cook? Yes, I'm a good cook ~ No, I'm not a good cook

**independent**

Do you think that all the countries of the world should be independent? Yes, I think ... ~ No, I don't think ...

## origin

Do many European languages have their origins in Latin?
Yes, many European languages ...

## belong to

Why don't you take this book home with you after the lesson?
I don't take that book home with me ... because it doesn't belong to me

Who does that pen belong to?
This pen belongs to me

If a factory belonged to you, do you think you would be able to make a lot of money?
Yes, if a factory belonged to me, I think I would be able ...

## could          vice versa

**"Could" is the past of "can", but we can also use "could" instead of "would be able" in conditional sentences.**

What can we use instead of "would be able" in conditional sentences?
We can use "could" instead of ...

Give me an example, please.
If I was a bird, I could fly

324 Now I'm going to ask you some questions with "could" and you answer with "would be able", and vice versa.

If you were very, very tall, could you touch the ceiling?
Yes, if I were ..., would be able to touch ...

If you were a doctor, would you be able to help people who were ill?
Yes, if I were ..., I could help ...

If you were as strong as a horse, could you lift a man above your head with only one hand?
Yes, if I were ..., I would be able to lift a man above my head ...

## throw

What am I going to do?
You're going to throw your pen at the window

Do you think you could throw a stone further than I can? Yes, I think I could ... further than you can ~ No, I don't think I could ... further than you can

### alive dead

Is Napoleon alive? No, Napoleon isn't alive; he's dead

### drop go without

What am I doing? You're dropping your pen on the table

What's the pen doing? The pen's dropping on the table

325 What would happen if I dropped a glass on the floor? If you dropped ..., it would break

What's the longest (time) you have ever gone without drinking a drop of water? The longest I've ever ... is ...

### assassinate

What happened to President Kennedy? President Kennedy was assassinated (in 1963)

### usual unusual

Did anything unusual happen to you yesterday? Yes, something unusual happened to me yesterday ~ No, nothing unusual happened to me yesterday

What?

Is it usual for people in your country to eat hot food for breakfast? Yes, it's usual for people in my country ... ~ No, it isn't usual for people in my country ...

Is it unusual for children to find coffee tasty? Yes, it's unusual ...

### still yet in progress

**We use "still" for something that is in progress at the moment, whereas we use "yet" for something that has not begun or happened.**

**For example, "It is still winter; it isn't spring yet. It is still 20...; it isn't 20... yet. It is still Monday; it isn't Tuesday yet" etc.**

**We generally use "still" in positive sentences, whereas we generally use "yet" in questions and negative sentences, but not always. We must learn when to use "still" and when to use "yet" by practice.**

326 What's the difference between "still" and "yet"?

The difference between "still" and "yet" is that we use "still" for something that is in progress at the moment, whereas we use "yet" for something that has not begun or happened. We generally use "still" in positive sentences, whereas we generally use "yet" in questions and negative sentences

Give me some examples, please.

It's still winter; it isn't spring yet

Has the lesson finished yet?

No, the lesson hasn't finished yet; it's still in progress

Have we finished speaking yet?

No, we haven't finished speaking yet; we're still speaking

Have they gone home yet?

No, they haven't gone home yet; they're still here

Has the spring (summer etc.) begun yet?

No, the spring (summer etc.) hasn't begun yet; it's still ...

Will I still be in this country in two weeks' time?

Yes, you'll still be ...

## special

*Dictation 37*

If I receive a call from him,/ I'll stay./ It is an ordinary paint factory;/ it makes nothing special./Rainy days make me sad./ I listened,/ but could hear no sound. What song do you suggest/ we get him to give us/ if he is not too tired?/ We don't turn right/ until we get to the next street./ The opposite of death is life.

*Do Revision Exercise 24*

# LESSON 63

327 **clean** **dirty** **dirt** **know of**

Are the bottoms of your shoes clean? No, the bottoms of my shoes aren't clean; they're dirty

When our shoes are dirty, what should we do? When our shoes are dirty, we should clean them

Which do you think is the cleanest city you know of? I think ... is the cleanest city I know of

And which do you think is the dirtiest? I think ... is the dirtiest

Which do you think is less unpleasant: the dirt of the city or the dirt of the country, of the farm etc.? I think the dirt of the ... is less unpleasant than the dirt of the ...

**to be afraid**

Do you remember if you were afraid of the dark when you were a little child? Yes, I remember I was afraid of the dark when I was a little child ~ No, I don't remember if I was afraid of the dark when I was a little child

Would you be afraid to go round the world in a small, open boat? Yes, I would be afraid ... ~ No, I wouldn't be afraid ...

Do people shake when they feel very afraid? Yes, people shake ...

328 **guard** **on your guard** **off your guard**

What's the best way to guard against becoming ill? The best way ... is to eat healthy food, sleep well and do exercise

Must we be on our guard when we buy something from a man selling things in the street? Yes, we must be ...

Why? Because maybe we won't be able to find him again if there's a problem with the thing we've bought

What's the opposite of "on your guard"? The opposite of "on your guard" is "off your guard"

**calm** **quietly**

What's the best way to calm somebody down when he's very angry? The best way ... is to speak quietly and pleasantly to him

Are we having calm weather at the moment? Yes, we're having ... ~ No, we aren't having ...

**if I were** **king**

**person** (1st, 2nd person etc.)

**In the 2nd conditional, we can use the verb "to be" in the past simple and say "if I was", "if you were", "if he was" etc. or we can use "were" for all persons and say "if I were", "if you were", "if he were" etc. The second form is perhaps more common.**

What are the two ways of forming the 2nd conditional with the verb "to be"? The two ways of forming the 2nd conditional with the verb "to be" are "if I was" and "if I were"

329 If you were a millionaire, where would you live? If I were ..., I would live in ...

Why?

If I were you, which language would I speak? If you were me, you would speak ...

If you were a king, what would your wife be called? If I were a king, my wife would be called a queen

If there wasn't a light in this room, would we be able to see well when it got dark? No, if there wasn't ..., we wouldn't ...; we would see badly

If there weren't any food in the world, would we all die? Yes, if there weren't ..., we would all die

If you weren't you, who would you like to be? If I weren't me, I would like to be ...

Why?

**if I were you advice expression especially**

**We say "If I were you" when we want to give advice to somebody, especially when we think perhaps there is a problem. For example, "If I were you, I would go to see a doctor" or "I wouldn't open that door if I were you!"**

Can we use the expression "if I were you" to give advice to somebody?
Yes, we can use the expression ...

Give me an example, please
"If I were you, I would eat more vegetables" or "I wouldn't buy that car if I were you!"

330 What's the biggest problem in your life at the moment?
The biggest problem in my life at the moment is ...

Give him/her some advice, please.
If I were you, I would ...

**win – won – won lottery**

What's another opposite of the verb "lose" besides "find"?
Another opposite ... is "win"

What are the three forms of "win"?
The three forms of "win" are "win, won, won"

Does your country usually win at football?
Yes, my country ... ~ No, my country ...; it usually loses

Do you do the lottery?
Yes, I do the lottery ~ No, I don't do the lottery

Have you ever won?
Yes, I've won ~ No, I've never won

If you won a million pounds, what would you do with it?
If I won ..., I would ...

**useful useless possess**

Is this pen useless?
No, this pen isn't useless; it's useful

What do we do with useless things?
We throw useless things away

What are the two most useful things you possess?
The two most useful things I possess are ...

331 **Do you think that what you're learning now will be useful to you later on in life?**

Yes, I think that what I'm learning now will be useful to me later on in life

**Why?**

Because it will help me get work, and speak to people from other countries

## take by surprise

*Dictation 38*

In the struggle,/ the enemy were surrounded/ at great speed/ and were taken by surprise/ without their swords/ in their hands./ I won't buy him/ a newspaper again./ Fetch me the salad bowl, please./ He is sorry that he sold his old house,/ which was in a quiet road./ The house he has now/ is in a very noisy street,/ and so he must try/ and find another,/ if possible.

# LESSON 64

332 **Contraction of "would"** **contract**

**The contraction of "I would" is "I'd". We can use contractions for all the persons and say "I'd", "you'd", "he'd", "she'd", "it'd", "we'd", "you'd", they'd".**

What's the contraction of "I would"? The contraction of ...

What are the contractions of "you would", "he would", "she would" etc.? The contractions of "you would", "he would", "she would" etc. are "you'd", "he'd, "she'd", "it'd", "we'd", "you'd", "they'd"

**From now on I want you to always use the contractions when speaking.**

If you went to the cinema this evening, which film would you see? If I went ..., I'd see ...

If I were you, which language would I speak? If you were me, you'd speak ...

If a plant had no water, would it die? Yes, if a plant ...

**Contraction of "would" with other words**

**We can contract "would" with almost any word. For example, "the book would" becomes "the book'd"; "who would" becomes "who'd" etc.**

What's the contraction of "book would"? The contraction of "book would" is "book'd"

333 lesson would; who would; what would; which would lesson'd; who'd; what'd; which'd

If you were a king, what'd your wife be called? If I were a king, my wife'd be called a queen

If you lost your way in a large city, who'd you ask? If I lost my way ..., I'd ask a policeman

If today were Sunday, what'd tomorrow be? If today were Sunday, tomorrow'd be Monday

**sandwich** **cheese**

When office workers are too busy to leave their desks for lunch, do they often just have a quick sandwich?
Yes, when office workers ...

What kind of things do we put in sandwiches?
We put meat, cheese, egg etc. in sandwiches

**fault** **faultless** **faulty**

**fix**

What's your biggest fault?
My biggest fault is ...

If your computer was faulty, would you know how to fix the fault?
Yes, if my computer was faulty, I'd know ...
~ No, if my computer was faulty, I wouldn't know ...

Are your dictations usually faultless?
No, my dictations aren't usually faultless; they usually contain mistakes

If a student makes a mistake in his dictation, is it usually his fault or the teacher's fault?
If a student ..., it's usually his fault, but it could sometimes be the teacher's fault

334 **OK** **all right**

**"OK" and "all right" have the same meaning.**

What can we say instead of "OK"?
Instead of "OK" we can say "all right"

**compare** **comparison**

**have something in common**

Can we compare Michelangelo with Napoleon?
No, we can't compare ...

Why not?
Because they were two completely different kinds of people, who did different things from each other

What must two people or things have if we want to make a comparison between them?
If we want to make a comparison between two people or things, they must have something in common

**ice** **cool**

What do we use ice for? We use ice for putting in drinks to cool them etc.

**pour**

What am I doing? You're pouring some water (wine etc.) from a bottle into a glass

335 **unite**

Do you think that all the countries of the world will unite one day? Yes, I think ... ~ No, I don't think ...

**even** **surprising**

**The word "even" can have a similar meaning to "also", but we use it when the next piece of information is surprising.**

Give me a sentence with "even" in it. She speaks Russian, German, French, and even Chinese ~ He was very impolite; he didn't even say "hello" ~ It's very simple; even a child could understand it

**mix** **mixture** **pink**

Do we generally mix sugar with potatoes? No, we don't generally ...

Do you think a mixture of tea and coffee would make a pleasant drink? No, I don't think ...; it would make an unpleasant drink

If you mixed some red and white paint together, what would you get? If I mixed ..., I'd get pink paint

**care** **care for** **take care of**

Who cared for you when you were a child? My mother cared for me when I was a child

336 Do you think the young should take care of the old? Yes, I think ...

Do you take good care of your health? Yes, I take good care of my health ~ No, I don't take good care of my health

Do you care what people think or say about you? Yes, I care ... about me ~ No, I don't care ... about me

## appointment keep an appointment hurry

## take your time

If you were late for a very important appointment, would you take your time? No, if I were ..., I wouldn't take my time; I'd hurry

Why? Because it's important to keep appointments that we've made

Why is it sometimes a bad thing to hurry? It's sometimes ... because we often make mistakes when we hurry

Would you take your time going home if somebody told you your house was on fire? No, I wouldn't take my time going home if somebody told me my house was on fire; I'd hurry

What's the translation of "I am in a hurry"? The translation of "I am in a hurry" is "..."

## plenty of

**The words "plenty of" mean "more than enough".**

What do the words "plenty of" mean? The words "plenty of" ...

337 Do people hurry when they have plenty of time? No, people don't hurry ...; they take their time

What's the opposite of "plenty of water"? The opposite of "plenty of water" is "little water" or "not enough water"

*Do Revision Exercise 25*

# LESSON 65

338 **for** **since** **period** **point**

**We came into this room at (six o'clock). The time now is (half past six). Therefore, we have been in this room for (half an hour). We have been in this room since (six o'clock).**

**We use the word "for" when we say a period of time. For example, "for half an hour"; "for two weeks"; "for six months"; "for ten years" etc. We use the word "since" when we say the point at which the period began. For example, "since six o'clock"; "since last Monday"; "since January"; "since 2002" etc.**

What's the difference between "for" and "since"?

The difference between "for" and "since" is that we use the word "for" when we say a period of time, whereas we use the word "since" when we say the point at which the period began

Give me some examples of "for".

for half an hour; for two weeks

Now give me some examples of "since".

since six o'clock; since last June

How long have you been in this room for?

I've been in this room for ...

Since when has he/she been in this room?

He's/She's been in this room since ...

How long have you lived in this town for?

I've lived in this town for ...

Since when has he/she lived in this town?

He's/She's lived in this town since ...

339 About how long have you known me for?

I've known you for about ...

Since when has he/she known me?

He's/She's known you since ...

Have you been able to speak English for more than ten years?

Yes, I've been able to ... ~ No, I haven't been able to ...

Have you been able to speak English since you were a young child?

Yes, I've ... since I was ... ~ No, I haven't ... since I was ...

**kitchen** **fridge** **freezer** **cooker**

**sink** **microwave**

What kind of things does a kitchen usually contain? A kitchen usually contains a fridge, a freezer, a cooker, a sink etc.

Does meat last longer in a fridge or a freezer? Meat lasts longer ...

Why do some people like using microwaves? Some people ... because they cook food very quickly

**studies**

Did you find English pronunciation a little difficult at the beginning of your studies? Yes, I found ... of my studies

Do you hope your English studies will help your future career?

Yes, I hope my ... my future career

340 **lend – lent – lent** **return**

Would you lend me some money if I asked you? Yes, I'd lend you some money if you asked me ~ No, I wouldn't lend you any money if you asked me

If you lent something to somebody and they didn't return it, what'd you do? If I lent something ..., I'd ...

**first name** **surname**

What's your first name? My first name's ...

What's your surname? My surname's ...

**actor** **actress** **famous** **film star**

Would you like to be famous? — Yes, I'd like ... ~ No, I wouldn't like ...

What's a film star? — A film star is a famous actor or actress in the cinema world

Tell me the names of some famous film stars, please. — Johnny Depp, Penelope Cruz etc.

Name a few famous people in history? — A few famous people in history are Shakespeare, Einstein, Michelangelo etc.

341 **industrial** **agricultural** **region**

What's the most industrial city in your country? — ... is the most industrial city in my country

What's the most agricultural region of your country? — ... is the most agricultural region of my country

**apologize** **apology**

**keep somebody waiting**

What do we say when we apologize for doing something wrong? — When we apologize ..., we say "I'm sorry"

If you keep somebody waiting for a long time, should you apologize? — Yes, if you keep ..., you should apologize

What's the noun of the verb "apologize"? — The noun ... is "apology"

**avoid**

How can we help to avoid becoming ill? — We can help ... by living a healthy life

**bend**

Do you have to bend down if you want to touch your feet? — No, I don't ... if I want to touch my feet, but it would be the easiest way

342 **century**

Which do you think was the best century in history to live in?

I think the ... century was the best ...

**fashion**

Do you like the fashion in clothes at the moment?

Yes, I like ... ~ No, I don't like ...

**gate**

Does this school have a gate outside it?

Yes, this school has ... ~ No, this school doesn't have ...

**worry** **be worried**

Do some people worry too much?

Yes, some people ...

Are you worried about your future?

Yes, I'm worried about my future ~ No, I'm not worried about my future

Why should you not worry if you don't immediately understand some of the grammar in this book?

I shouldn't worry if I don't ... because I will practise it again in other lessons, and I can study it at home

**run**

When we're in a hurry, what must we do?

When we're ..., we must run

343 What's the furthest you've ever run?

The furthest I've ever run is ...

*Dictation 39*

Comedy films make us laugh./ He won't offer his cigarettes round/ when he is in company./ On cloudy days,/ she prefers to stay inside./ We had to work very hard yesterday/ and weren't very pleased about it,/ because it was a lovely, sunny day./ The car came round the bend/ in the road/ at top speed./ The driver was able/ to avoid the bike/ that was coming the other way,/ but went straight into the gate/ on the other side.

# LESSON 66

344 **Past continuous** | **I was speaking**

**particular** | **while**

**We use the present continuous for an action that is in progress now. For example, "I am speaking English now".**

**We use the past continuous for an action that was in progress at a particular time in the past. For example, "I was speaking English at this time yesterday". If I say "I was sleeping at 4 o'clock this morning", it means that I went to sleep before 4 o'clock and I woke up after 4 o'clock; at 4 o'clock, I was in the middle of a period of sleeping.**

When do we use the present continuous? — We use the present continuous for an action that is in progress now

Give me an example, please. — I am speaking English now

When do we use the past continuous? — We use the past continuous for an action that was in progress at a particular time in the past

Give me an example, please. — I was speaking English at this time yesterday

**The most common use of the past continuous is to say that an action was in progress when another action happened. For example, "I was cooking lunch when she arrived" means that, when she arrived, I was in the middle of cooking lunch.**

Were you chatting to anybody when I came into the room at the beginning of the lesson? — Yes, I was ... when you ...; ~ No, I wasn't ... when you ...

345 Were the students standing or sitting when I left the classroom at the end of the last lesson? — The students were ... when you left the classroom ...

Was it raining while you were coming to school today? Yes, it was raining while I was coming ... ~ No, it wasn't raining while I was coming ...

What were you doing at this time last Sunday? I was ... at this time last Sunday

Do you think most people in this town were sleeping at midnight last night? Yes, I think ...

Where were you living ten years ago? I was living ... ten years ago

### earn

About how much does a doctor earn a year in your country? A doctor earns about ... a year in my country

### formal informal jeans trainer

### how do you do?

Would it be OK for a man to wear jeans and trainers if he was going to a formal dinner? No, it wouldn't be ...; he should wear a suit and tie

When we meet somebody for the first time, what can we say? When we meet ..., we can say "Nice to meet you"

And what do we say if we want to be more formal? If we want ..., we say "How do you do?"

And what does the other person reply? The other person replies "How do you do?"



### persuade

Is it easy to persuade people to give their money away? No, it isn't easy ...; it's difficult

### hairdresser

How often do you go to the hairdresser's? I go to the hairdresser's ... times a year

**so** **interesting** **exciting**

Why do you think some films are so popular? I think ... because they tell interesting or exciting stories

**grammatically**

Is it grammatically correct to say "I've seen her yesterday"? No, it isn't ...; we should say "I saw her yesterday" instead

**bathroom** **bath** **shower**

**toilet** **basin**

What does a bathroom usually contain? A bathroom usually contains a bath or shower, a toilet and a basin

Which do you prefer: baths or showers? I prefer ...

What's a rain shower? A rain shower is a short period of rain

347 **mirror** **reflect**

What does a mirror do? A mirror reflects light

In which rooms in a house do we usually find a mirror? We usually find a mirror in a bathroom or a bedroom

## Active and passive voice

**active** **passive**

**subject** **object**

### Active voice

### John broke the window

**In the sentence "John broke the window", "John" is the subject and "the window" is the object. The verb, "broke", is in the active voice. All the verbs we have practised up to now have been in the active voice. The**

**active voice communicates that the subject is active and it does the action in the sentence.**

## Passive voice

## The window was broken by John

**This sentence, "The window was broken by John", has the same meaning, but the subject is now "The window", and the verb, "was broken", is in the passive voice. The passive voice communicates that the subject is passive; it does not do the action; it receives it.**

348 **"To be" + past participle by**

**We form the passive voice with the verb "to be" and a past participle. The verb "to be" communicates the time, and the past participle says what the action is. We use the word "by" when we want to say who does the action.**

**In the sentence "The window was broken by John", the word "was" tells us that the action happened in the past, the word "broken" tells us the action, and the words "by John" tell us who did the action.**

| | |
|---|---|
| What does the active voice communicate? | The active voice communicates that the subject does the action |
| What does the passive voice communicate? | The passive voice communicates that the subject receives the action |
| How do we form the passive voice? | We form the passive voice with the verb "to be" and a past participle |
| Give me some examples, please. | My car was washed last month.<br>Many computers are made in China.<br>The students will be taught by the teacher. |

**We must remember to put the verb "to be" in the right form. For example, "John has eaten pasta" becomes "Pasta has been eaten by John".**

Now I am going to give you a sentence in the active voice, and I want you to put it into the passive voice:

| | |
|---|---|
| John eats the pasta | The pasta is eaten by John |

**John ate the pasta** — The pasta was eaten by John

**John has eaten the pasta** — The pasta has been eaten by John

349 **John will eat the pasta** — The pasta will be eaten by John

**John is eating the pasta** — The pasta is being eaten by John

**John was eating the pasta** — The pasta was being eaten by John

**John would eat the pasta** — The pasta would be eaten by John

**Now we're going to practise with some different sentences:**

**I clean my car every Saturday** — My car is cleaned by me every Saturday

**She forgot him** — He was forgotten by her

**My boss is going to write that email** — That email is going to be written by my boss

**We are fixing the car** — The car is being fixed by us

**They have followed all the advice** — All the advice has been followed by them

*Dictation 40*

They could perhaps meet/ a friend of theirs/ on their way home/ after the lesson./ He had a bad cold,/ but he refused/ to take any medicine./ You can learn words and grammar/ by reading books/ or using the internet./ However, you cannot learn/ how to speak a language well/ without practising it./ We must, therefore,/ try to speak/ as often as possible./ Do you have enough time/ to finish the work?

*Do Revision Exercise 26*

# LESSON 67

350 **force** **make somebody do ...**

Do I force you to give long answers during the lesson?
Yes, you force me/us to give ...

Why? Because it is important to speak as much as possible

**In the construction "make somebody do ...", the word "make" means "force" or "cause". For example, "The teacher made me correct my dictation" means that he forced me to correct my dictation. The sentence "Sunny weather makes me feel happy" means that it causes me to feel happy.**

When you were a child, did your parents make you eat your vegetables?
Yes, when I was a child, my parents ...
~ No, when I was a child, my parents didn't ...

What kind of films make you laugh? The kind of films that make me laugh are ...

**snack** **break** **biscuit** **crisps**

What is a snack? A snack is something small that people eat between meals, like a sandwich or a bag of crisps

Which would you prefer as a snack during a morning break: a bag of crisps or some biscuits? I'd prefer ...

**to be born**

Where were you born? I was born in ...

351 How soon after you were born did you learn to walk? I learnt to walk about a year after I was born

**murder**

Do you like reading books with stories about murders in them?
Yes, I like ... ~ No, I don't like ...

## prison

Would you like to see inside a prison? Yes, I'd like ... ~ No, I wouldn't like ...

Why or why not? Because I'd find it interesting ~ Because it'd make me feel very unhappy

## pupil

What's a pupil? A pupil is a child who's in school

Do most pupils in your country have to wear a uniform? Yes, most pupils in my country ... ~ No, most pupils in my country don't ...

## root

What do we call the part of a tree that's in the land? We call the part ... the roots

## memory

Have you got a good memory? Yes, I've got ... ~ No, I haven't got ...

## 352 Another contraction of the verb "to be"

| | | | |
|---|---|---|---|
| I'm | not | I'm | not |
| you | aren't | you're | not |
| he | isn't | he's | not |
| she | isn't | she's | not |
| it | isn't | it's | not |
| we | aren't | we're | not |
| you | aren't | you're | not |
| they | aren't | they're | not |

**Instead of "I'm not", "you aren't", "he isn't" etc., we can use "I'm not", "you're not", "he's not" etc.**

What can we use instead of "I'm not", "you aren't", "he isn't" etc.?
Instead of "I'm not", "you aren't", "he isn't" etc., we can use "I'm not", "you're not", "he's not", "she's not", "it's not", "we're not", "you're not", "they're not"

## cross

If you want to go from one side of the road to the other, what must you do?
If I want ..., I must cross the road

What must you do before crossing the road?
I must look both ways before ...

353 If you wanted to go from here to Scotland, would you have to cross the sea or would you be able to go all the way by land?
If I wanted ..., I'd ...

## think of

What was the first thing you thought of when you woke up this morning?
The first thing I thought of when I ... was ...

## safe safety on your own

What's the opposite of the word "dangerous"?
The opposite ... is "safe"

Do you think it's safe to shop online?
Yes, I think ... ~ No, I don't think ...

Do parents often worry about their children's safety?
Yes, parents often ...

Is it safe for young children to cross the road on their own?
No, it isn't ...

Do you like going on holiday on your own?
Yes, I like ... on my own ~ No, I don't like ... on my own; I prefer going in company

## lay

What's the past of the verb "to lie"?
The past of ... is "lay"

How long did you lie in bed for last night?
I lay in bed for ... hours last night

354 **sir** **madam** **gentleman** **lady**

**customer** **officer**

**To be polite, people who work in shops, hotels etc. use the words "sir", "madam" or "miss" when they speak to customers. Also, in the army, a soldier calls his officer "sir", and at school, a pupil sometimes calls his teacher "sir" or "miss".**

When do people use the words "sir" and "madam"?

People use ... to be polite when they are speaking to their customers in a shop, their officers in the army, or their teachers at school

Give me an example, please.

"Excuse me sir; can I help you?"

**When we want to sound polite, we can use the words "gentleman" and "lady" instead of "man" and "woman". For example, we can say "Who is that gentleman over there?" or "The lady I spoke to on the phone yesterday told me to call again today".**

When do we use the words "gentleman" and "lady"?

We use ... instead of "man" and "woman" when we want to sound polite

Give me an example, please.

"Which of these two gentlemen gave you the book?" and "Will you ask that lady her name, please?"

**title**

**Everybody has a title. For most people, it is "Mr", "Mrs", "Miss" or "Ms". For example, John Brown's title is "Mr", so we call him "Mr Brown". The title "Mrs" is for married women; the title "Miss" is for unmarried women; the title "Ms" can be used for either married or unmarried women.**

355 **Some people have other titles, such as "Sir" and "Lady". For example "Sir Paul McCartney" and "Lady Diana".**

What's your title?

My title is "..."

Give me examples of "Sir" and "Lady" used as titles.

Some examples ... are "Sir Paul McCartney" and "Lady Diana"

**standard** **height**

**Which two countries have the highest standards of living in the world?**

... and ... have the highest standards of living in the world

**What's the standard height for a man (or woman) in this country?**

The standard height ... is ...

**colourful**

*Dictation 41*

Sixteenth century fashions/ in men's clothes/ were very colourful./ The word "use" is a verb,/ whilst the word "use" is a noun./ After the verb "succeed",/ we use the word "in"/ followed by a gerund./ For example,/ "He succeeded in answering the question."/ He is only a beginner,/ but believes he will succeed./ I hope so./ A hard worker/ rarely fails an examination,/ so students should always work hard.

# LESSON 68

356 **would you say** **opinion**

**We use the expression "would you say" when we ask somebody for his opinion about something. It means "Do you think ... ?"**

When do we use the expression "would you say"?
We use the expression ...

Would you say that a king's life was better than that of the average man?
Yes, I'd say ... ~ No, I wouldn't say ...

**Notice that we use the past tense after "would you say", because it is part of a conditional construction.**

Which tense do we use after the expression "would you say"?
We use the past tense after ...

What would you say was the best way to remember something?
I'd say that the best ... was to repeat it often

**"Look" + adjective**

If the sky looks dark and cloudy, do you sometimes decide not to go out?
Yes, if the sky ..., I sometimes ...

When your shoes look dirty, what do you do?
When my shoes ..., I clean them

357 **get in** **get out of**

**get on** **get off** **taxi** **fare**

**We get in/into a car, but we get on/onto a bus, a train, a plane or a ship.
We get out of a car, but we get off a bus, a train, a plane or a ship.**

Do we pay the driver when we get in a taxi?
No, we don't ...; we pay when we get out of a taxi

In your country, do you have to buy a ticket before getting on a bus?

Yes, in my country, you have to ... ~ No, in my country, you don't have to ...; you can just pay when you get on

How much is the bus fare from here to where you live?

The bus fare ... where I live is ...

**royal**

Has your country got a royal family?

Yes, my country's got ... ~ No, my country hasn't got ...

**mud** **countryside**

How do we get mud on our shoes?

We get mud ... by walking in the countryside in the rain

**crowd** **crowded**

Are famous actors often surrounded by crowds when they go out in public?

Yes, famous actors are ...

Are the buses in this town usually crowded in the morning?

Yes, the buses ... ~ No, the buses ...

358 **captain** **team**

Have you ever been the captain of a sports team?

Yes, I've been ... ~ No, I've never been ...

Tell me the name of a famous sea captain.

The name of ... is Captain Cook/Nemo etc.

**wide** **narrow**

Which is the widest street in the place where you live, and which is the narrowest?

... is the widest street in ..., and ... is the narrowest

**flag** **national**

What colour is the flag of your country?

The flag of my country is ...

Do you know the origin of your national flag?

Yes, I know ... ~ No, I don't know ...

**grass** **live on**

**If we say "John lives on pasta", we mean that John only eats pasta.**

Name an animal that lives on grass. A horse is an animal ...

What happens to grass if there's no rain? If there's no rain, grass becomes yellow and then it dies

359 **tower**

Where is the nearest tower to the place where you live? The nearest tower ... I live is ...

**wet** **dry**

Are the streets dry when it rains? No, the streets aren't ...; they're wet

If you walked in the rain without an umbrella, what'd happen? If I walked ..., I'd get wet

If you got wet, what'd you have to do with your clothes? If I got wet, I'd have to take my clothes off and hang them up to dry

**threw**

What's the past of "throw"? The past of "throw" is "threw"

What'd happen if I threw a stone at the window? If you threw ..., the window'd break

**loud** **turn up** **turn down**

If your TV is turned up too loud, what do you do? If my TV ..., I turn it down

360 **Reflexive pronouns**

**myself** **yourself** **himself**

**herself** **itself** **oneself**

**ourselves** **yourselves** **themselves**

**consequently** **protect**

**We use a reflexive pronoun when the subject and object are the same person or thing. In the sentence "The teacher taught me", the subject and the object are different people. In the sentence "I taught myself", the subject and the object are the same person. Consequently, we use the reflexive pronoun "myself" as the object.**

What are the reflexive pronouns? — The reflexive pronouns are "myself", "yourself", "himself", "herself", "itself", "oneself", "ourselves", "yourselves" and "themselves"

When do we use a reflexive pronoun? — We use a reflexive pronoun when the subject and object are the same person or thing

Is it right to say "I looked at me in the mirror"? — No, it isn't right ...

Why not? — Because the subject and object are the same person

What must we say instead? — We must say "I looked at myself in the mirror" instead

Do you think it'd be easy for me to teach myself Chinese (Arabic etc.)? — No, I don't think ... for you to teach yourself ...

Why not? — Because ... is a difficult language to learn

361 Did you wash yourself when you were a baby? — No, I didn't wash myself when I was a baby; my mother washed me

What'd you do if you saw a man trying to kill himself? — If I saw ..., I'd try to stop him or call the police

Have you ever seen a bird washing itself? — Yes, I've seen ... ~ No, I've never seen ...

Do you think one can teach oneself a language? — Yes, I think ... ~ No, I don't think ...

What do we carry to protect ourselves from the rain? — We carry an umbrella to protect ...

*Do Revision Exercise 27*

# LESSON 69

362 **thorough** **thoroughly**

What does the word "thorough" mean? The word "thorough" means "complete"

In which season of the year do people generally give their houses a thorough cleaning? People generally ... in spring

If you jumped into the sea, would you get thoroughly wet? Yes, if I ..., I'd get ...

What kind of things make you thoroughly tired? The kind of things that make me thoroughly tired are hard physical work, studying a lot without a break, not enough sleep etc.

**accident** **by accident**

If you drove a car on the left-hand side of the road (in America, France etc.) instead of on the right, what'd happen? If I drove ..., I'd have an accident

Have you ever seen an accident on the road? Yes, I've seen ... ~ No, I've never seen ...

If you took something by accident that didn't belong to you, what'd you do? If I took ... to me, I'd return it

363 **careful** **careless** **carefully** **carelessly**

Do people become careless when they're in great danger? No, people don't ...; they become very careful

Do you write carefully? Yes, I write ... ~ No, I don't ...; I write carelessly

What could happen if you were careless when crossing the road? If I were ..., I could have an accident

Of all the people you know, who dresses the most carelessly? Of all the people I know,

... dresses the most carelessly

### own

**Do you own all the clothes you're wearing, or do any of them belong to somebody else?**

I own ... I'm wearing ~ I don't own ... I'm wearing; some of them belong to somebody else

**What would you like to own more than anything else?**

I'd like to own ... more than anything else

**Who owns the place where you live?**

... own(s) the place where I live ~ I don't know who owns the place where I live

### carry on retire

**Do people in your country usually carry on working after they reach the age of 65?**

Yes, people in my country ... ~ No, people in my country ...; they retire

### 364 prize

**Have you ever won a prize for anything?**

Yes, I've won a prize for something ~ No, I've never won a prize for anything

**What?**

### too

**Give me a sentence with the word "too", meaning "also".**

He wants a biscuit, and I want one too

### at least

**Give me a sentence with the words "at least" in it.**

I've asked him at least six times, and each time he has forgotten ~ He didn't do very well in the exam, but at least he passed

### widely

**Which is one of the most widely used English adjectives?**

One of the ... is "nice" ("good" etc.)

Is English the most widely spoken language in the world? Yes, English is ...

**manner** **pig**

Why are good manners so important in life? Good manners are ... because they make life easier and more pleasant

365 What do we mean when we say that somebody has the manners of a pig? When we say ..., we mean that they have very bad manners

Do people in very hot countries dress in the same manner as people in very cold countries? No, people in ...; they dress in a different manner

**asleep** **awake**

Will you still be asleep at 11 o'clock tomorrow morning? No, I won't still be ...; I'll be awake

Will you still be awake at 3 o'clock tomorrow morning? No, I won't still be ...; I'll be asleep

**hospital** **nurse**

Who takes care of us when we're in hospital? Nurses and doctors take ...

**purpose** **in order to ...** **so that**

**take exercise**

**The most common way to communicate purpose in English is by using the infinitive with "to". For example, the sentence "I went to the hospital to see a doctor" tells us the purpose of going to the hospital. With formal English, it is more common to use "in order to". For example, we would say "I visited the hospital in order to see a doctor".**

366 Answer the following questions with "in order to":

Why do people eat? People eat in order to live

For what purpose do people work? People work in order to earn money

What must we do in order to keep in good health? In order to ..., we must sleep well, eat healthy food, take plenty of exercise, not smoke etc.

What do you think is the purpose of living? I think the ... is to be happy and to make others happy etc.

**We can also use "so that" to communicate purpose. For example, "She shut the door so that the cat could not go into the garden".**

Give me an example of "so that", please. He put the food in the fridge so that it would stay fresh

## notice

Are there any notices hanging up in the school? Yes, there are some ... ~ No, there aren't any ...

Where?

What do they say?

## lain

What are the three forms of "lie"? The three forms of "lie" are "lie, lay, lain"

What's the longest you've ever lain in bed for when you've been ill? The longest I've ever ... when I've been ill is about ...

## 367 point at point out indicate

**We use "point at" for the action of pointing the finger at an object. For example, "I'm pointing at that picture". However, "to point out" means to indicate something among different things. For example, "He pointed out the mistakes in my dictation".**

**What's the difference between "to point at" and "to point out"?**

The difference between "to point at" and "to point out" is that we use "to point at" for the action of pointing the finger at an object, whereas "to point out" means to indicate something among different things

**What am I doing?** — You're pointing at the light

**Point at the picture on the wall, please.**

**What are you doing?** — I'm pointing at ...

**Point out the mistake in this sentence, please: "I've gone to the cinema this week".**

We can't say "I've gone ..."; we must say "I've been to the cinema this week"

**What's he doing?** — He's pointing out the mistake in that sentence

## grave

**In your country, do people visit their relatives' graves?**

Yes, in my country, people ... ~ No, in my country, people ...

## 368 neck

**Is it bad for your neck to sleep without a pillow?** — Yes, it's bad ... ~ No, it isn't bad ...

## flame

**Can we have a fire without flames?** — Yes, we can ...

## flight

**How long is the flight from here to ...?** — The flight from ...

**soup** **except**

*Dictation 42*

The flag on top of the tower/ is wide at one end/ and narrow at the other./ Thin soup is very pleasant,/ but I prefer a big bowl/ of thick soup/ when I'm hungry./ Except for me,/ nobody knew that our actions/ were against the law./ He gets angry/ when he loses his way/ and has to ask a policeman./ I'll continue swimming/ until I feel tired./ Fish can't stay alive/ without water.

# LESSON 70

369 **may** **might** **palace**

**parliament**

**The words "may" and "might" both express the idea of "perhaps", but we cannot use "may" in the 2nd conditional. For example, we cannot say "If I was rich, I may buy a big house "; we must say "I <u>might</u> buy" instead.**

What do the words "may" and "might" express? The words "may" and "might" express the idea of "perhaps"

What's the difference between "may" and "might"? The difference between "may" and "might" is that we cannot use "may" in the 2nd conditional

Give me an example. If I went to London, I might visit Buckingham Palace

Do you think it may rain later? Yes, I think it may rain later ~ No, I don't think it will rain later

What do you think I might have in my pocket? I think you might have ... in your pocket

What might happen if you didn't look both ways before crossing the road? An accident might happen if I didn't ...

What might you see if you went to London? I might see Buckingham Palace, the Houses of Parliament, Trafalgar Square, Piccadilly Circus etc. if I went to London

Do you think there might be another world war? Yes, I think there might be ... ~ No, I don't think there'll be ...

370 **arrive at** **point** **arrive in** **area**

**airport** **passport**

**We arrive <u>at</u> a point, like a building or a station, whereas we arrive <u>in</u> an area, like a city or a country.**

What's the difference between "arrive at" and "arrive in"?
The difference between "arrive at" and "arrive in" is that we arrive at a point, whereas we arrive in an area

What time do you arrive at school?
I arrive at school at ...

If you arrived at a foreign airport without your passport, what might happen?
If I arrived ... without my passport, I might not be able to enter the country

## café

What is a café?
A café is a small, informal restaurant where you can get light meals, snacks and drinks

## owe

Do you owe me any money?
Yes, I owe you some money ~ No, I don't owe you any money

Do I owe you any money?
Yes, you owe me some money ~ No, you don't owe me any money

## Verb + back

## souvenir

**When we add the word "back" to a verb it means "to return". For example, "give back", "go back", "pay back" etc.**

371 What does it mean "to give back"?
"To give back" means "to return"

When you go on holiday, what do you bring back with you?
When I go ..., I bring back souvenirs with me

Are you going to go back home immediately after the lesson's ended?
Yes, I'm going to go ... ~ No, I'm not going to go ...

When people lend you money, do you always pay it back when promised?
Yes, when people lend me money, I always ... ~ No, when people lend me money, I don't always ...

Do you know anybody who has retired but then later gone back to work?
Yes, I know somebody ... ~ No, I don't know anybody ...

**pride** **proud** **normal** **normally**

**take pride in**

What is your normal breakfast? My normal breakfast is ...

Do people normally feel proud when they do well in exams? Yes, people normally ...

Do you take pride in your work (studies)? Yes, I take pride in my work (studies) ~ No I don't take pride in my work (studies)

**servant**

If you were very rich, would you have servants in your house? Yes, if I were ..., I'd have servants in my house ~ No, if I were ..., I wouldn't have servants in my house

372 **wheel** **lorry**

Does a lorry have fewer wheels than a car? No, a lorry doesn't ...; it has more wheels

**arrow** **centimetre** **metre**

About how long is an arrow? An arrow is about a metre long

How many centimetres make a metre? A hundred centimetres make a metre

**beard**

Do you know anybody who has a long beard? Yes, I know somebody ... ~ No I don't know anybody ...

**true** **false** **paper (newspaper)**

Is it false that the opposite of "heaven" is "hell"? No, it isn't false ...; it's true

Is everything we read in the newspapers true? No, not everything ...; some things are true and some things are false

Why do you think this is so? — I think maybe it's because newspapers haven't always got time to make sure that what they write is completely true

**maintain**

Is it cheap to maintain a large house? — No, it isn't cheap ...; it's expensive

373 **it takes** **Ireland**

How do we translate the words "it takes"? — We translate ... with "..."

How long does it take you to go home from here? — It takes me about ... to go ...

Does it take longer to fly from here to Ireland than to go by train and ship? — No, it doesn't take ...; it takes less time

About how long would it take us to reach the station from here if we walked very fast? — It'd take us about ... to reach ...

**amount** **amount to**

What amount of money have you got in your pocket (or bag) at the moment? — I've got about ... in my pocket ...

Do they use a large amount of wood in building houses in this region? — Yes, they use ... ~ No, they don't use ...

Why or why not? — Because it's cheap/expensive etc.

What do £50 and £13 amount to? — £50 and £13 amount to £63

**further** **Sweden** **in addition**

**extra**

**The word "further" means the same as "farther", but it also means "in addition" or "extra".**

What does the word "further" mean? — The word "further" ...

374 **Which is further from Spain: Sweden or Switzerland?**
Sweden is further from Spain than Switzerland

**What's the furthest you've ever been?**
The furthest I've ever been is from ... to ...

**Where'd you have to go if you wanted further information about train times at a station?**
I'd have to go to the information office if I wanted ...

**Give me a further example of the word "further", please.**
If I failed an exam, I'd have to take further lessons

*Dictation 43*

They keep lots of their books/ under the bed./ She's pouring the fruit juice/ from a bottle into a glass./ His grave/ was covered with sand,/ and, in the sand,/ somebody had printed his name./ From the neck of the bottle/ came a flame/ which gave light to the room./ Fish and chips/ is a common meal in England./ If we push a door/ which has the word "pull"/ written on it,/ it won't open./ He's got a hole in his sock.

*Do Revision Exercise 28*

# LESSON 71

375 **Past perfect** **I had eaten**

**The past perfect communicates the same idea as the present perfect except that, instead of thinking about time before and up to now, we are thinking about time before and up to a specific point in the past. For example, with the present perfect, we can say "Mary cannot enter her flat because she has lost her key". With the past perfect, we can say "Mary could not enter her flat yesterday because she had lost her key".**

When do we use the present perfect?
We use the present perfect when we are thinking about time before and up to now

Give me an example.
Mary cannot enter her flat because she has lost her key

What does that sentence mean?
That sentence means that Mary does not know where her key is now because of losing it earlier today

When do we use the past perfect?
We use the past perfect when we are thinking about time before and up to another point in the past

Give me an example.
Mary could not enter her flat yesterday because she had lost her key

What does that sentence mean?
That sentence means that Mary did not know where her key was yesterday because of losing it earlier in the day

376 What's the difference between these two sentences?

"I ate my dinner at 9 o'clock"

and

"I had eaten my dinner at 9 o'clock"

The difference between these two sentences is that "I ate my dinner at 9 o'clock" means I started to eat my dinner at 9 o'clock, whereas "I had eaten my dinner at 9 o'clock" means that my dinner was already finished at 9 o'clock

Had you had anything to eat before you came to school today?
Yes, I had had something ... before I came ...
~ No, I hadn't had anything ... before I came ...

Had you ever seen me before you came to this school?
Yes, I had seen you before I came ...
~ No, I had never seen you before I came ...

When you began your lessons at this school, had you already studied some English or were you a complete beginner?
When I began my lessons ..., I had already ...
~ When I began my lessons ..., I hadn't studied any English; I was a complete beginner

**party** **political**

What does the word "party" mean?
The word "party" means ...

Do you ever throw (have) a party at home on your birthday?
Yes, I sometimes ... on my birthday ~ No, I never ... on my birthday

Which is the strongest political party in your country today?
The ... party is the ... in my country today

Do you prefer to go on holiday with a friend or in a large party?
I prefer to go on ...

377 **mad** **crazy** **UFO**

**The word "mad" has three common meanings: angry, very interested, and crazy.**

What does the word "mad" mean?
The word "mad" means angry, very interested, and crazy

Do some people get mad when they're driving in very heavy traffic?
Yes, some people ...

What kind of things are you most mad about?
I'm most mad about music, films, sport etc.

If a friend told you they had seen a UFO, would you believe them or think they were going mad?
If a friend told me ..., I'd ...

## copy

What happens if one pupil copies from another during an exam?

If one pupil ..., he's sent out of the room

When you answer a question during a Callan lesson, should you simply copy what the teacher says?

No, when I answer ..., I shouldn't simply ...; I should try to answer the question without waiting to hear the words from the teacher first

If you were given two copies of the same book for your birthday, what would you do?

If I were given ... for my birthday, I'd ...

378 ## influence

Does the weather have a strong influence over you? Do you, for example, feel happy in good weather and unhappy in bad weather?

Yes, the weather ... over me
~ No, the weather ... over me

## mouse mice

What is the name of the famous mouse in the cinema world?

The name of ... is Mickey Mouse

What do mice like eating?

Mice like eating cheese etc.

## throat

What part of the body's this?

It's the throat

## opportunity

Which would you prefer: a job that gave you the opportunity to visit other countries, or a job that gave you the opportunity to earn a lot?

I'd prefer a job that gave me the opportunity to ...

**develop** **industry** **agriculture**

What do we mean by the under-developed countries of the world?
By the under-developed ..., we mean those with little industry, agriculture etc.

379 **print**

Where was this book printed? This book was printed in ...

**sand** **beach** **desert**

Where do we find sand? We find sand on a beach, in a desert etc.

When you're on holiday, do you enjoy lying on a beach in the sun?
Yes, when I'm ..., I enjoy ...
~ No, when I'm ..., I don't enjoy ...

Why is it difficult to live in a desert? It's difficult ... because there is so little water

**bell** **knock** **pay a visit** **ring**

What am I doing? You're knocking on the table

Is there a bell in this school? Yes, there's a bell ...
~ No, there isn't a bell ...

What do you do when you arrive at somebody's front door in order to pay a visit? When I arrive at ..., I knock on the door or ring the doorbell

**shout**

When do people shout? People shout when they're angry or when they think somebody can't hear them

If there were some people shouting loudly outside in the corridor, would you be able to hear me? No, if there were ..., I wouldn't be able to hear you

**stick** **walking stick**

Do some people use walking sticks to help them move around when they get older? Yes, some people ...

Which animals like to fetch sticks that you throw for them? Dogs like to fetch ...

## Would prefer + infinitive with "to"

Where would you prefer to live: by a lake or by the sea? I'd prefer to live by ...

This evening, would you prefer to go out for dinner or simply go home? This evening, I'd prefer to ...

**exclamation mark**

*Dictation 44*

Keep off the grass!/ They've gone away for the day/ and will return late/ this evening;/ at least, that's what they said/ before leaving./ The average age/ for getting married/ is between twenty and thirty./ Among all the subjects/ I studied at school,/ I found science/ the most interesting,/ not the most boring./ Birds cannot fly/ faster than planes./ The soldiers carried the sticks/ into the field/ in order to make a fire.

# LESSON 72

381 **-ness** **reason**

**illness** **tiredness** **darkness**

**To form a noun from an adjective, we sometimes add the letters "ness" to the adjective. For example, "slow – slowness", "late – lateness", "careless – carelessness" etc.**

How do we sometimes form a noun from an adjective? — We sometimes form a noun from an adjective by adding the letters "ness" to the adjective

Give me an example. — late – lateness

When did you have your last illness? — I had my last illness ...

What's the reason for tiredness? — The reason for tiredness is too much work, not enough sleep etc.

What's the reason for darkness at night? — The reason for darkness at night is that the world turns completely round every 24 hours

**alone**

What's another way of saying "he lives on his own"? — Another way ... is "He lives alone"

Do you live alone or with other people? — I live alone ~ I live with other people

Do you prefer to go on holiday alone? — Yes, I prefer ... ~ No, I don't prefer ...; I prefer to go in company

382 **already**

Has the lesson already finished? — No, the lesson hasn't finished yet; it's still in progress

Are you already able to speak English without making any mistakes? — No, I'm not able to ... yet; I still make some mistakes

Are we already in spring (summer etc.)?

No, we aren't in ... yet; we're still in ...

Have we already studied Stage 4 of the Callan Method?

Yes, we've already studied ...

## thrown

What are the three forms of "throw"?

The three forms of "throw" are "throw, threw, thrown"

Have you ever thrown anything away by mistake which was worth a lot of money?

Yes, I've thrown something away ... ~ No, I've never thrown anything away ...

What?

## in spite of / despite

**"In spite of" and "despite" both mean the same as "although", but they are prepositions, so we put nouns after them.**

**There are three ways of using "in spite of" or "despite". They can be followed by a noun, or "-ing", or "the fact that ...". For example:**

**In spite of her illness, she went to work.**

**Despite being ill, she went to work.**

**In spite of the fact that she was ill, she went to work.**

383 **It is important to remember that "in spite of" and "despite" cannot be followed immediately by a subject and verb. For example, we <u>cannot</u> say "In spite of she was ill, she went to work".**

Why do some people do dangerous sports in spite of the danger?

Some people ... because they find them exciting

Name some foods that are very popular despite being bad for the health.

Some foods that are very ... are ...

Do you think it's worth learning a foreign language in spite of the fact that it's quite difficult?

Yes, I think ...

In spite of studying a lot of words and grammar, do you still find English a little difficult?

Yes, in spite of ..., I still find ...

## anyone someone no one (no–one)

**Instead of the words "anybody", "somebody" and "nobody", we can use the words "anyone", "someone" and "no one" (or "no-one").**

What words can we use instead of "anybody", "somebody" and "nobody"?
Instead of "anybody", "somebody" and "nobody", we can use "anyone", "someone" and "no one"

Did anyone come into the classroom at the beginning of the lesson?
Yes, someone came ...

Who went out of this room two minutes ago?
No one went ...

384 **borrow**

What's the opposite of the verb "to lend"?
The opposite ... is "to borrow"

Should we always give back the things we borrow?
Yes, we should always ...

If you forgot to bring a pen with you to school, would you have to borrow one from another student?
Yes, if I forgot ... with me to school, I'd have to ...

## my own emphasize

**We often put the word "own" after a possessive adjective when we want to emphasize that something belongs to someone. For example, this is my own pen; it belongs to me. Notice that we can say that this is <u>our</u> classroom because we study here all the time, but we cannot say that this is <u>our own</u> classroom because it doesn't belong to us.**

Give me an example of the word "own" after a possessive adjective.
This is my own book

Do you live in your own house (or flat), or does it belong to somebody else?
Yes, I live in my own house (or flat) ~ No, I don't live in my own house (or flat); it belongs to ...

Do you think this is probably my own book or do you think it belongs to the school?
I think that's probably your own book ~ I don't think that's your own book; I think it belongs ...

**skin**

What's this? — It's your skin

385 **wire** **electricity**

**connection** **wireless** **Wi–Fi**

**hyphen**

What do we use wire for? — We use wire to carry electricity, to connect things together etc.

What do we mean by a wireless internet connection? — By a wireless internet connection, we mean that we can connect to the internet without connecting wires to our computer

What can we say instead of "a wireless internet connection"? — Instead of ..., we can say "Wi-Fi"

Do some bars and cafés offer free Wi-Fi to their customers? — Yes, some bars ...

Spell the word "Wi-Fi", please. — W, I, hyphen, F, I

**boil** **fry** **roast**

Tell me three ways of cooking potatoes. — Three ways ... are boiling, frying and roasting

Do you prefer fried eggs or boiled eggs? — I prefer ...

How long does it take to boil potatoes? — It takes about twenty minutes to boil potatoes

**brick**

What's a wall normally built of? — A wall is normally built of bricks

## as well too also

**The words "as well", "too" and "also" all mean the same thing. The words "as well" and "too" go at the end of the sentence, but the word "also" usually goes after the first auxiliary verb.**

Where do the words "as well", "too" and "also" usually go?

The words "as well" and "too" go at the end of the sentence, but the word "also" usually goes after the first auxiliary verb.

Give me an example of each, please.

I will be sleeping at 3 a.m.; my sister will be sleeping as well; my mother will be sleeping too; my brother will also be sleeping.

**With the present simple and past simple, there is no auxiliary in the positive, so the word "also" simply goes between the subject and the verb. For example, we say "He speaks German and he also speaks French".**

Give me an example of "also" when there is no auxiliary verb, please.

I love coffee and I also love tea

*Do Revision Exercise 29*

# LESSON 73

387 **Future continuous** **I will be speaking**

**We use the future continuous for an action that will be in progress at a particular time in the future. For example, the sentence "I will be sleeping at 4 o'clock tomorrow morning" means that I will go to sleep before 4 o'clock and I will wake up after 4 o'clock; at 4 o'clock, I will be in the middle of a period of sleeping.**

When do we use the future continuous? — We use the future continuous ...

Give me an example, please. — I will be working at this time tomorrow

What do you think you will be doing at this time tomorrow? — I think I'll be ... at this time tomorrow

Will you still be studying English in fifty years' time? — No, I won't still be studying ...

Where do you think you'll be living in ten years' time? — I think I'll be living ... in ten years' time

**inch** **foot** **yard**

**This is an inch; this is a foot; this is a yard. An inch is about two-and-a-half centimetres. Twelve inches make a foot, and three feet make a yard. A yard is about three inches shorter than a metre.**

What's this? — It's an inch

388 What's this? — It's a foot

What's this? — It's a yard

How many centimetres make an inch? — About two and a half centimetres make an inch

How many inches make a foot? — Twelve inches make a foot

How many feet make a yard? — Three feet make a yard

Is a yard longer than a metre? No, a yard ...; it's shorter than a metre

Consequently, when we run a hundred yards, do we run further than a hundred metres? No, when we run ...; we run less than ...

## chain

Are you wearing a chain? Yes, I'm ... ~ No, I'm not ...

What do we mean when we say someone is a chain-smoker? When we say ..., we mean that he or she smokes one cigarette after another without stopping, like a chain

## rise constantly

What's my book doing? Your book's rising in the air

Does the sun rise early in winter? No, the sun doesn't ...; it rises late

Is the cost of living constantly rising these days? Yes, the cost of living is ... ~ No, the cost of living isn't ...

389 What'd you do if this table slowly began to rise into the air without anybody touching it? If this table ..., I'd run out of the room etc.

## belt

Are you wearing a belt? Yes, I'm ... ~ No, I'm not ...

## hourly daily weekly monthly yearly

**The words "hourly", "daily", "weekly", "monthly" and "yearly" mean "every hour", "every day", "every week", "every month" and "every year".**

What do the words "hourly", "daily", "weekly", "monthly" and "yearly" mean? The words "hourly", "daily" ... mean "every hour", "every day" ...

Do most radio stations have hourly traffic news? Yes, most radio stations ...

Which daily newspaper do you read? I read ...

Do you read any weekly newspapers? Yes, I read some ...
~ No, I don't read any ...

Which?

How many hours of English do you study monthly? I study ...
hours of English monthly

Where do you usually go for your yearly holidays? I usually go ...
for my yearly holidays

390 **allow** **let – let – let** **everyday**

**The verbs "allow" and "let" have the same meaning. The difference is that "allow" has the infinitive with "to" after it, whereas "let" has the infinitive without "to" after it. For example, we can say "The policeman allowed the man to go home" or "The policeman let the man go home". In everyday English, "let" is more common than "allow".**

What's the difference between "allow" and "let"?
The difference between "allow" and "let"
is that "allow" has the infinitive with "to" after it,
whereas "let" has the infinitive without "to" after it

Give me an example, please. The doctor allowed
me to change my appointment.
The doctor let me change my appointment.

What sometimes happens when we let people borrow things that belong to us? When we let ..., they sometimes don't return them

Do you think it's a good idea to allow children to do as they please (want to)? No, I don't think ...

Do you think it's dangerous these days to let people we don't know enter our houses? Yes, I think ... ~ No, I don't think ...

Do you think more people would kill each other if the law of the country let them? Yes, I think ... ~ No, I don't think ...

**Another difference between "allow" and "let" is that we cannot use "let" in the passive voice. We cannot say "I was let"; we must say "I was allowed".**

**Which is it right to say: "I was let" or "I was allowed"?** It's right to say "I was allowed"

**Why?** Because we cannot use "let" in the passive voice

**Do you think students should be allowed to use their mobile phones during lessons?** Yes, I think ... ~ No, I don't think ...

391 *Dictation 45*

From over the lake/ came the sound/ of the church bells. /The fat man swam/ better than his thin friend./ She lost her way/ and was unable to find a policeman./ Some past participles of verbs are:/ begun, known, swum,/ taken, shaken, written,/ forgotten and broken./ We use the word "whether"/ to express a doubt./ The only way to learn/ how to cook/ is by practice.

# LESSON 74

| | | |
|---|---|---|
| 392 | **Anywhere?** | **somewhere**<br>**not anywhere** |
| | Where? | on the wall<br>**nowhere** |

Is there a book anywhere in this room? Yes, there's a book somewhere in this room

Is there a radio anywhere in this room? No, there isn't a radio anywhere in this room

If there's nowhere to sit on a bus, what do you have to do? If there's nowhere ..., I have to stand

Is there anywhere near here I can buy foreign books? Yes, there's somewhere near here you can ...

Is there anywhere in this town I could get my hair cut for nothing? No, there isn't ... you could get your hair cut for nothing

Where in the world can a man murder another man without breaking the law? There's nowhere in the world ...

If you could live anywhere in the world, where would you live? If I could live ..., I'd live in ...

Why?

393 **loose** **loosen**

Do you think it's OK to let dogs run around loose, or do you think they should be kept on a chain? I think it's OK ... ~ I think dogs should ...

Why do people in hot countries wear loose clothes? People in hot countries ... to keep themselves cool

Are there any loose stones on the road outside this school? Yes, there are some ... ~ No, there aren't any ...

Why does a man sometimes loosen his tie? A man sometimes ... because it's more comfortable

**storm** **lightning** **thunder**

What's a storm? A storm is a short period of very bad weather

What do we sometimes see and hear in a storm? We sometimes see lightning and hear thunder in a storm

**blind**

How do blind people read? Blind people read with special books made for them, which they can read by touching the words

**devil**

Where does the devil live? The devil lives in hell

394 **ride** **cycle**

Can you ride a horse? Yes, I can ... ~ No, I can't ...

Do you like riding on buses? Yes, I like ... ~ No, I don't like ...

What's another way of saying "I ride a bike every day"? Another way ... is "I cycle every day"

**may** **can** **could** **permission**

**When we ask for permission to do something, we use the words "may", "can" or "could". For example, "May I leave the room, please?"**

What words do we use when we ask for permission to do something? We use "may", "can" or "could" when we ask ...

Give me three examples, please. May I smoke? Can I open the window? Could I borrow your pen, please?

**catch** **raincoat**

**We use the word "catch" in expressions such as "catch a ball", "catch a train", "catch a cold" etc.**

In what kind of expressions do we use the word "catch"?
We use the word "catch" in expressions such as ...

What am I doing?
You're throwing your pen into the air and catching it

395 Are you the kind of person who usually has to run hard at the last moment in order to catch a bus or a train?
Yes, I'm the kind of ... ~ No, I'm not the kind of ...

If you walked in the rain without carrying an umbrella or wearing a raincoat, what might happen?
If I walked ..., I'd get wet and might catch a cold

## cap

Why is it a good idea to wear a cap in hot, sunny weather?
It's a good idea ... because it protects your head and eyes from the sun

## habit — be in the habit of doing

**The most common way to speak about our habits is to use the present simple or past simple. For example, we say "I drink coffee every day" or "I usually went to bed early when I was a child". We sometimes add expressions like "usually", "always" or "every week" so that it is understood that we are speaking about a habit.**

What's the most common way to speak about our habits?
The most common ...

Give me an example, please.
I play football every weekend. I always studied hard before exams at university

Does your father smoke?
Yes, my father smokes ~ No, my father doesn't smoke

Did you usually go to bed early when you were a small child?
Yes, I usually went to bed early when I was ...

What's your worst habit?
My worst habit is that I (smoke, drink too much coffee etc.)

**Notice that we can also say that someone is "in the habit of doing" something.**

396 Are you in the habit of speaking to yourself when you're alone?

Yes, I'm in the ... to myself when I'm alone
~ No, I'm not in the ... to myself when I'm alone

What were you in the habit of doing at the weekend when you were a little child?

I was in the habit of ... at the weekend when I was ...

## stranger foreigner

**A stranger is somebody we don't know, whereas a foreigner is somebody from another country.**

What's the difference between a stranger and a foreigner?

The difference between a stranger and a foreigner is that a stranger is ...

## snowstorm

*Dictation 46*

Don't shout all the time!/ I can hear you/ well enough/ when you speak quietly./ However,/ the best way to learn anything in English/ is by practice./ They've always kept their promises,/ so they say./ Of course he finds life boring;/ he watches the same television programmes/ all the time./ They were nearly blinded/ by the snowstorm,/ and could not see which direction/ the ambulance was coming from.

*Do Revision Exercise 30*

# LESSON 75

397 **look like**

What famous person would you most like to look like? I'd most like to look like ...

What does he/she look like? He/She is ... and has ...

Do you look more like your mother or your father? I look more like my ...

Do you think it looks like rain (or looks as if it is going to rain)?
Yes, I think ... ~ No, I don't think ...

Do you think you look like succeeding (or look as if you will succeed) in learning English quite well? Yes, I think I look ...

**travel** **journey** **just**

**The difference between "travel" and "journey" is that we generally use "travel" as a verb and "journey" as a noun. For example, "I travelled a long way" or "The journey was long".**

What's the difference between "travel" and "journey"?
The difference between ...

Why is it now easier for people to travel to other countries just for the weekend? It's now easier ... because travelling is cheaper and faster these days

398 What's the longest journey you've ever made? The longest journey I've ever made is from ... to ...

**of course**

Give me a sentence with the words "of course" in it, please.
Could I borrow your pen for a second? Of course you can ~ He's American and so, of course, he speaks English

## nowadays

Do you think people are happier nowadays than they were in the past?
Yes, I think ... ~ No, I don't think ...

Why or why not?

## suffer

Have you suffered from any illnesses in the last two years?
Yes, I've suffered from some illnesses ...
~ No, I haven't suffered from any illnesses ...

## wish

What's your greatest wish in life? My greatest wish in life is ...

## exist

About how long has this building existed for? This building has existed for ...

399 **remind** **in other words** **member**

**The difference between the words "remember" and "remind" is that we remember something ourselves, without help, whereas, if we forget something, somebody reminds us. In other words, they remember for us.**

What's the difference between the words "remember" and "remind"?
The difference between ...

If you forget the meaning of a word during the lesson, who reminds you of it? If I forget ..., the teacher reminds me of it

If you have an important appointment to keep, which member of your family reminds you to keep it? If I have ..., my ... reminds me ...

Do I remind you of any member of your family? Yes, you remind me of ... ~ No, you don't remind me of any ...

**library**

What's the difference between a bookshop and a library?
The difference ... is that a bookshop is a place where we can buy books, whereas a library is a place where we can go to read books and borrow them

**even though** **even** **not even**

When you were a child, did you sometimes have to go to school even though you didn't want to?
Yes, when I was a child, I sometimes had to ... I didn't want to

400 Are there some areas of the world where it never gets warm, even in the middle of summer?
Yes, there are ...

Will there be even more people and more cars in the world in a few years' time?
Yes, there'll be ...

Do you know of a village in this country where they haven't even got water or electricity?
Yes, I know of ... ~ No, I don't know of ...

Where?

**to** **at** **direction**

**The difference between the words "to" and "at" is that we generally use "to" when we are moving in the direction of a place, and "at" when we are there. For example, "I'm going to the table. Now, I'm (standing) at the table".**

What's the difference between the words "to" and "at"?
The difference between ...

Give me an example, please.
I'm going to the table, and now I'm at the table

Are you coming to the school?
No, I'm not ...; I'm at the school

Am I going to the table?
No, you aren't ...; you're (standing) at the table

**soon** **at once**

**If I go out of the room and say "I'll be back soon", how long will I be?**
If you go ..., you'll be maybe five or ten minutes

**If I go out of the room and say "I'll be back at once", how long will I be?**
If you go ..., you'll be about one minute, or you'll be back almost immediately

401 **Will it soon be spring (summer, autumn, or winter)?** Yes, it'll soon be ...

**Is the lesson going to finish soon?** Yes, the lesson's ... ~ No, the lesson isn't ...

**How soon do you think it will be before everybody in the world has enough money in order to live a comfortable life?** I think it'll be a long time before everybody ...

**Which would get you home sooner: a bus or a car?** I think maybe a car would get me home sooner than a bus

# LESSON 76

402 **need**

What would you do if you needed a haircut? — If I needed ..., I'd go to a hairdresser's

What do you think you need more than anything else in your life? — I think I need ... more than anything else in my life

What do you think your country needs more than anything else? — I think my country needs ... more than anything else

**towards** **destination**

**The word "towards" means "in the direction of". For example, if I say "I'm walking towards the station" it means that I'm walking in the direction of the station; it doesn't necessarily mean that the station is my destination.**

What does the word "towards" mean? — The word "towards" means ...

What am I doing? — You're walking towards the door

If I tell you that I am driving towards Scotland, does that necessarily mean that Scotland is my destination? — No, if you tell me that you are ..., that doesn't necessarily mean that Scotland is your destination

403 **tray**

What do we use a tray for? — We use a tray for carrying plates and cups from one room to another

**stadium**

Where is the nearest sports stadium? — The nearest ...

About how many people does it hold? — It holds ...

**much better** **much more**

**If we put the word "much" before a comparative, it communicates that the difference between the two things is very big. For example, Germany is bigger than England, but China is much bigger than England.**

Why do you speak English much better now than you did six months ago?
I speak English ... than I did six months ago because I've had much more practice

Why is a Rolls Royce much more expensive than an ordinary car?
A Rolls Royce is ... because it takes longer to make than an ordinary car

**contrary** **fall**

**temperature** **atmosphere**

What's another word for "opposite"?
Another word for "opposite" is "contrary"

What's the contrary of the verb "to rise"?
"To fall" is the contrary ...

404 Is the temperature of the atmosphere falling this month?
Yes, the temperature ... ~ No, the temperature ...; it's rising

If your body temperature falls a lot, what should you do?
If my body temperature ..., I should go to bed and call a doctor

**tooth** **teeth** **toothbrush** **dentist**

What's the plural of "tooth"?
The plural of "tooth" is "teeth"

What do we clean our teeth with?
We clean our teeth with a toothbrush

If you have a problem with your teeth, who should you go to see?
If I have ... with my teeth, I should go to see a dentist

**seem**

Does it seem to you as if it'll rain later?
Yes, it seems to me as if ... ~ No, it doesn't seem to me as if ...

Why do some people seem younger than they really are?
Some people seem ... because of the way they look, the way they talk, the things they do etc.

Does it seem warmer to you today than it was yesterday?
Yes, it seems warmer to me...
~ No, it doesn't seem warmer to me ...

## several

Are you ill several times during the year?
Yes, I'm ill ...
~ No, I'm not ill ...

405 Do some very rich people have houses in several different countries?
Yes, some very ...

## compose

## be composed of

Did Mozart compose a lot of music?
Yes, Mozart composed ...

Do you find it difficult to compose formal letters?
Yes, I find it ...
~ No, I don't find it ...; I find it easy

How many letters is the English alphabet composed of?
The English alphabet is composed of 26 letters

Is Europe composed of many different countries?
Yes, Europe's composed of ...

## wise

## wisdom

Do you agree that it's wise to put some money in the bank each month for later on in life?
Yes, I agree ...; No, I don't agree ...

Do you think wisdom comes more with age or experience?
I think wisdom comes more with ...

## suddenly

If I suddenly threw my pen at you, would you be able to catch it?
Yes, if you ... your pen at me, I'd ...
~ No, if you ... your pen at me, I wouldn't ...

## pain

**What's the greatest physical pain you've ever suffered?**

The greatest ... I've ever suffered was ...

406 **certain**

**Is there anything in life that we can be completely certain of?**

Yes, there's ... ~ No, there isn't ...

**What?**

## pass by

**From where you're sitting can you see people passing by the window?**

Yes, from where I'm sitting, I can ...
~ No, from where I'm sitting, I can't ...

## park car park

**When a car park is full, where does a driver have to park his car ?**

When a ..., a driver ... in the street

## picture

*Dictation 47*

Instead of a belt/ she wore a chain,/ which was the fashion of the day./We usually picture the devil/ as having long ears/ that become thin and narrow/at the top./ The word "great" generally means very good,/ but it can also mean/ big or important./ "Fast" means the same as "quick",/ except that/ we do not add "ly" to it/ as an adverb.

*Do Revision Exercise 31*

# LESSON 77

407 **3rd Conditional**

**Before we think about the 3rd conditional, we should remind ourselves of the 1st conditional and 2nd conditional:**

**1st Conditional**

**"If" + present + "will do" = real possibility**

**If I go to the park tomorrow, I will play football**

**2nd Conditional**

**"If" + past + "would do" = only imagining**

**If I went to the park tomorrow, I would play football**

When do we use the 1st conditional? We use the 1st conditional to communicate that we think something is a real possibility in the future

What is its construction? Its construction is "If" + present + "will do"

Give me an example, please. If he sees his friend this evening, he will say "Hello"

408 When do we use the 2nd conditional? We use the 2nd conditional to communicate that we are only imagining something

What is its construction? Its construction is "If" + past + "would do"

Give me an example, please. If she went to the North Pole next week, she would feel very cold

## 3rd Conditional

### "If" + past perfect + "would have done" = imagining in the past

### If I had gone to the park yesterday, I would have played football

**We use the 3rd conditional to communicate that we are imagining something in the past that did not really happen. Its construction is "If" + past perfect + "would have done". The sentence "If I had gone to the park yesterday, I would have played football" means that, in fact, I did not go to the park yesterday, and I did not play football; I am only imagining.**

When do we use the 3rd conditional? — We use the 3rd conditional when we are imagining something in the past that did not really happen

What is its construction? — Its construction is "If" + past perfect + "would have done"

Give me an example, please. — If she had studied harder, she would have succeeded in the exam last month

**Notice that, in the 3rd conditional, we put the word "have" and the past participle after the word "would". For example, we say "I would have taken"; "you would have taken"; "he would have taken" etc.**

409 In the 3rd conditional, what do we put after the word "would"? — In the 3rd conditional, we put the word "have" and the past participle after the word "would"

Give me some examples, please. — He would have slept. She would have written. They would have eaten.

If you had been born in England, which language would you have spoken as a child? — If I had been ..., I would have spoken English as a child

Were you in fact born in England? — No, I wasn't in fact ...; I was born in ...

**Exactly; we are only imagining.**

Did you find £100 on the street yesterday? — No, I didn't ...

But if you had found £100 on the street yesterday, what would you have done with it?

If I had ..., I would have kept it/taken it to the police station

If you had not decided to study English, which language would you have studied instead?

If I had not ..., I would have studied ... instead

If you had not come to school last week, what would you have done instead?

If I had not ..., I would have gone on holiday/stayed at home etc.

## diary

What do people use diaries for?

People use diaries to help them remember things that they have done or things that they need to do

## 410 character

What kind of character do you like to see in a person?

I like to see a ... character in a person

## really

Have you ever got up really early?

Yes, I've sometimes ... ~ No, I've never ...

For what reason?

If you were driving a car on a long journey and suddenly felt really tired, what would you do?

If I were ..., I'd stop the car, buy a cup of coffee, and wait until I felt more awake

## ran

What's the past of "run"?

The past of ... "ran"

If you ran against him (or me etc.), who do you think'd win?

If I ran ..., I think ... would win

## improve

## coach

How can we improve our English?

We can ... by practising a lot, reading a lot etc.

Why do even the best tennis players need a coach? Even the best ... to help them to improve their game

Is it cheaper to travel by coach or by train in your country? It's cheaper ... in my country

## 411 Adverbs formed from adjectives

**As you have already seen, one very common way of forming adverbs is by adding the letters "ly" to the adjective. For example, "careful – carefully"; "dangerous – dangerously"; "useless – uselessly" etc.**

Tell me one very common way of forming adverbs from adjectives? One very common way ...

Give me some examples, please. bad – badly; quick – quickly etc.

### flew

What's the past of "fly"? The past of "fly" is "flew"

If you flew round the world in a straight line, would you finish in the same place as you had started? Yes, if I flew ..., I'd finish in ...

If a bird flew into this room, what'd you do? If a bird ..., I'd probably try to catch it

### wool

Which animal do we get wool from? We get wool from a sheep

What can we make from wool? We can make pullovers, hats and scarves from wool

## 412 Possessive case of plural nouns ending in "s"

### apostrophe case

How do we form the possessive case of singular nouns like "girl", "man", "child" etc.? We form the possessive case of ... by adding an apostrophe and the letter "s"

Give me some examples, please. The girl's coat; the old man's hat; a child's book

How do we form the possessive case of plural nouns that do not end in "s", such as "men", "women", "children" etc.? We form the possessive case of ... in the same way: by adding an apostrophe and the letter "s"

Give me some examples, please. The old men's hats; children's books; women's clothes

**When, however, a plural noun already ends in "s", we form its possessive case just by adding an apostrophe, but no "s".**

How do we form the possessive case of a plural noun which already ends in "s"? We form the possessive case of ... just by adding an apostrophe, but no "s"

Give me some examples, please. The girls' coats; the workers' clothes; ladies' dresses

What do footballers' shirts have written on their backs? Footballers' shirts have numbers written on their backs

### kick

What am I doing? You're kicking the table

413 **coast** **certain**

Can the English coast be seen from the coast of France? Yes, on certain days, the English coast ...

### tire

Do you ever tire of speaking? Yes, I sometimes tire ... ~ No, I never tire ...

## *Dictation 48*

What have they just done?/ They've just learnt that/ we use the 1st conditional/ to communicate that we think/ something is a real possibility./ Its construction is/ "if" + present + "will do"./ In the second conditional,/ we use the past tense to communicate/ that we are only imagining something./ We use "would"/ followed by the infinitive without "to"/ to talk about the imagined result.

## Revision Exercise 24 (Lessons 52 – 53)

1 Which do you prefer: cats or dogs?

2 Do people in your country think it's lucky to see a black cat?

3 Do you ever destroy documents that you receive from your bank?

4 Have you been to the cinema this week?

5 Have you ever been to Scotland?

6 If I take something from a shop without paying, am I guilty of a crime?

7 What's the opposite of "guilty"?

8 Have you visited Paris?

9 Are you too short to touch the ceiling?

10 If you work too much, do you feel tired all the time?

11 At what age did you begin school?

12 How much does the average meal cost in the average restaurant in the place where you live?

13 Is your book thinner than the glass in the window?

14 Is Switzerland a bigger country than India?

15 What's the difference between a purse and a wallet?

16 Which do you think it's worse to lose, your keys or your purse/wallet?

17 Do you find English easy to learn?

18 What kind of things make you angry?

19 What does it mean "to swim like a fish"?

20 What do we call the two ends of a swimming pool?

### Answers

1 I prefer ...

2 Yes, people in my country think it's lucky to see a black cat. ~ No, people in my country don't think it's lucky to see a black cat; they think it's unlucky.

3 Yes, I sometimes destroy documents that I receive from my bank.

4 Yes, I've been to the cinema this week. ~ No, I haven't been to the cinema this week.

5 Yes, I've been to Scotland. ~ No, I've never been to Scotland.

6 Yes, if you take something from a shop without paying, you're guilty of a crime.

7 The opposite of "guilty" is "innocent".

8 Yes, I have visited Paris. ~ No, I haven't visited Paris.

9 Yes, I'm too short to touch the ceiling.

10 Yes, if I work too much, I feel tired all the time.

11 I began school at the age of ...

12 The average meal costs about ... in the average restaurant in the place where I live.

13 No, my book isn't thinner than the glass in the window; it's thicker.

14 No, Switzerland isn't a bigger country than India; it's a smaller country than India.

15 The difference between a purse and a wallet is that women generally have purses and men generally have wallets.

16 I think it's worse to lose my ...

17 Yes, I find English easy to learn. ~ No, I don't find English easy to learn; I find it difficult.

18 The kind of things that make me angry are when things go wrong, when people are making too much noise ... etc.

19 "To swim like a fish" means to be a strong swimmer.

20 We call the two ends of a swimming pool the shallow end and the deep end.

## Revision Exercise 25 (Lessons 54 – 55)

1 What do we call a bad dream?

2 Do you ever refuse to help other people?

3 Do you live in a separate house from your parents?

4 Do you agree it's very bad for the health to keep eating after our stomachs are completely full?

5 Do you keep your money in your pocket, or do you use a purse or wallet?

6 Do you keep books after you've read them?

7 What's the best way to keep warm on a cold day?

8 What do we sometimes mean when we use the words "one, you, we" and "they"?

9 What do you have to do if you want to stay healthy?

10 Which country must we go to if we want to hear people speaking Greek?

11 What's the difference between the present perfect and the past simple?

12 Have you been to the cinema this year?

13 When was the last time you went to the cinema?

14 Does your bank have a branch near here?

15 Are there any bridges over the river in Paris?

16 What subject interests you the most?

17 Are you interested in the history of your country?

18 Do you get bored if you have nothing to do?

19 What's the difference between "between" and "among"?

20 Among all the places you've ever been to, which do you think is the ugliest?

### Answers

1 We call a bad dream a nightmare.

2 Yes, I sometimes refuse to help other people. ~ No, I never refuse to help other people.

3 Yes, I live in a separate house from my parents. ~ No, I don't live in a separate house from my parents; I live in the same house.

4 Yes, I agree it's very bad for the health to keep eating after our stomachs are completely full.

5 Yes, I keep my money in my pocket. ~ No, I don't keep my money in my pocket; I use a purse/wallet.

6 Yes, I keep books after I've read them. ~ No, I don't keep books after I've read them.

7 The best way to keep warm on a cold day is to wear a thick coat.

8 When we use the words "one, you, we" and "they" we sometimes mean people in general.

9 If you want to stay healthy, you have to eat healthy food, sleep well and do exercise.

10 We must go to Greece if we want to hear people speaking Greek.

11 The difference between the present perfect and the past simple is that we use the present perfect when we are thinking about time before or up to now, whereas we use the past simple when we are thinking about a specific past time.

12 Yes, I've been to the cinema this year. ~ No, I haven't been to the cinema this year.

13 The last time I went to the cinema was ...

14 Yes, my bank has a branch near here. ~ No, my bank doesn't have a branch near here.

15 Yes, there are some bridges over the river in Paris.

16 ... interests me the most.

17 Yes, I'm interested in the history of my country. ~ No, I'm not interested in the history of my country.

18 Yes, I get bored if I have nothing to do. ~ No, I don't get bored if I have nothing to do.

19 The difference between "between" and "among" is that we generally use "between" for two people or things, whilst we use "among" for more than two people or things.

20 Among all the places I've ever been to, I think ... is the ugliest.

## Revision Exercise 26 (Lessons 56 – 57)

1 Do you think it's going to rain soon?

2 What kind of things do you enjoy doing most of all?

3 Do you always enjoy your weekends?

4 What kind of hole do we find in a door?

5 Which do you think are more intelligent: cats or dogs?

6 What's another word for "intelligent"?

7 Who does your town play football against?

8 What's the past participle of the verb "to go"?

9 Why can I say "Mr Brown has gone to Scotland", but not "I have gone to Scotland"?

10 Can a bird fly quicker than a plane (aeroplane)?

11 What's the difference between "thick" and "fat"?

12 Did you swim last summer?

13 Have you ever lost your way in a large city?

14 What's the difference between "each other" and "one another"?

15 Do your country and England play football against each other?

16 Do the countries of Europe do business with one another?

17 What's the past of "can"?

18 What's the future of "can"?

19 Tell me the names of some things that we make in factories.

20 Do soldiers wear ordinary clothes?

**Answers**

1 Yes, I think it's going to rain soon. ~ No, I don't think it's going to rain soon.

2 The kind of things I enjoy doing most of all are watching television, going to the cinema etc.

3 Yes, I always enjoy my weekends. ~ No, I don't always enjoy my weekends.

4 We find a keyhole in a door.

5 I think ... are more intelligent than ...

6 Another word for "intelligent" is "clever".

7 My town plays football against ...

8 The past participle of the verb "to go" is "gone".

9 I can say "Mr Brown has gone to Scotland", but not "I have gone to Scotland", because "I have gone to Scotland" means I am not here now, which is impossible.

10 No, a bird can't fly quicker than a plane; it flies slower than a plane (aeroplane).

11 The difference between "thick" and "fat" is that we use "thick" for things and "fat" for people and animals.

12 Yes, I swam last summer. ~ No, I didn't swim last summer.

13 Yes, I've sometimes lost my way in a large city. ~ No, I've never lost my way in a large city.

14 The difference between each other and one another is that we generally use "each other" for two people or things, and "one another" for more than two people or things.

15 Yes, my country and England play football against each other. ~ No, my country and England don't play football against each other.

16 Yes, the countries of Europe do business with one another.

17 The past of "can" is "could".

18 "Can" has no future. Therefore, we use the verb "to be able" and say "I will be able".

19 The names of some things that we make in factories are cars, pens etc.

20 No, soldiers don't wear ordinary clothes; they wear uniforms.

## Revision Exercise 27 (Lessons 58 – 59)

1 Can you understand all the words when you listen to a song in English?

2 What's the difference between the words "fun" and "funny"?

3 Have you had your lunch today?

4 What's the furthest you've ever swum?

5 Is it possible to learn English simply by listening to English songs?

6 Have you ever taken things that weren't yours by mistake?

7 What's the difference between these two sentences? "I'm going to buy the car if it's cheap" and "I'm going to buy the car whether it's cheap or not?

8 What is the highest speed a car can go when in town in this country?

9 Do you like unpleasant surprises?

10 Is it a big struggle for you to get up on a cold winter's morning when you feel very tired?

11 Do you think computers make your life easier or more difficult?

12 Do you turn off your computer when you go to bed at night?

13 Tell me the names of some great people in history.

14 What is the past simple and the past participle of the verb "to keep"?

15 Have you always kept your promises?

16 Did you find English very difficult when you began studying it?

17 Have you ever found anything on the street worth a lot of money?

18 Does anybody else in your family speak English besides you?

19 Is it easier to dance well if you have a good sense of rhythm?

20 When somebody makes you angry, do you say something or do you just stay quiet?

### Answers

1 No, I can't understand all the words when I listen to a song in English.

2 The difference between the words "fun" and "funny" is that, if something is fun, we enjoy it, whereas, if something is funny, it makes us laugh.

3 Yes, I've had my lunch today. ~ No, I haven't had my lunch today.

4 The furthest I've ever swum is ...

5 No, it isn't possible to learn English simply by listening to English songs.

6 Yes, I've sometimes taken things that weren't mine by mistake. ~ No, I've never taken things that weren't mine by mistake.

7 The difference between these two sentences is that the first sentence means I'm going to buy the car only if it's cheap, whereas the second sentence means I'm going to buy the car if it's cheap or expensive; the price is not important.

8 The highest speed a car can go when in town in this country is ...

9 No, I don't like unpleasant surprises.

10 Yes, it's a big struggle for me to get up on a cold winter's morning when I feel very tired.

11 I think computers make my life ...

12 Yes, I turn off my computer when I go to bed at night. ~ No, I don't turn off my computer when I go to bed at night.

13 The names of some great people in history are Mahatma Gandhi, Albert Einstein, Marie Curie etc.

14 The past simple and the past participle of the verb "to keep" is "kept".

15 Yes, I've always kept my promises. ~ No, I haven't always kept my promises; sometimes I've broken them.

16 Yes, I found English very difficult when I began studying it.

17 Yes, I've found something on the street worth a lot of money. ~ No, I've never found anything on the street worth a lot of money.

18 Yes, somebody else in my family speaks English besides me. ~ No, nobody else in my family speaks English besides me.

19 Yes, it's easier to dance well if you have a good sense of rhythm.

20 When somebody makes me angry, I ...

## Revision Exercise 28 (Lesson 60 – 61)

1 Is it probable that it will snow next summer?

2 When do we use the 1st conditional?

3. When do we use the 2nd conditional?
4. If you felt ill tomorrow, would you go out?
5. If you study hard, will you learn to speak English well?
6. If you had £1 million, what would you buy?
7. If you swam in the sea in the middle of winter, would you find the water warm?
8. If you go on holiday next year, where will you go?
9. If you found something in the street worth a lot of money, would you keep it or would you take it to the police station?
10. If you sent a letter and forgot to put the address on it, would it arrive?
11. Do you prefer chatting with your friends on the phone or online?
12. What's the first thing you notice about people when you meet them for the first time?
13. Is it more comfortable to sleep lying down or sitting up?
14. What was the first thing you saw when you woke up today?
15. If you went from London to Rome, which cities would you perhaps have to go through?
16. When a teacher puts a cross next to an answer in a written test, what does it mean?
17. Is it dangerous to drive after drinking alcohol?
18. What's the difference between these two sentences: "I must study" and "I should study"?
19. In a Callan Method lesson, does the teacher correct your grammatical mistakes?
20. If you have a problem with a colleague at work, should you speak to your boss about it?

**Answers**

1. No, it isn't probable that it will snow next summer; it's very improbable.
2. We use the 1st conditional to communicate that we think something is a real possibility.
3. We use the 2nd conditional to communicate that we are only imagining something.
4. No, if I felt ill tomorrow, I wouldn't go out; I would stay at home.
5. Yes, if I study hard, I will learn to speak English well.

6 If I had £1 million, I would buy ...
7 No, if I swam in the sea in the middle of winter, I wouldn't find the water warm; I would find it cold.
8 If I go on holiday next year, I will go to ...
9 If I found something in the street worth a lot of money, I would keep it/take it to the police station.
10 No, if I sent a letter and forgot to put the address on it, it wouldn't arrive.
11 I prefer chatting with my friends ...
12 The first thing I notice about people when I meet them for the first time is their voice (clothes, eyes etc.)
13 It's more comfortable to sleep lying down than sitting up.
14 The first thing I saw when I woke up today was ...
15 If I went from London to Rome, I would perhaps have to go through Paris, Milan etc.
16 When a teacher puts a cross next to an answer in a written test, it means the answer is wrong.
17 Yes, it's dangerous to drive after drinking alcohol.
18 The difference between those two sentences is that "I must study" means that I have no alternative, whereas "I should study" means I have alternatives but that studying is the right thing for me to do.
19 Yes, in a Callan Method lesson, the teacher corrects your grammatical mistakes
20 Yes, if I have a problem with a colleague at work, I should speak to my boss about it.

## Revision Exercise 29 (Lessons 62 – 63)

1 Do you think the lives of the poor are happier than those of the rich?
2 Although you're now able to hold a simple conversation in English, do you think you should keep studying?
3 Does your mum cook tasty food?
4 Give me a sentence with the words "such as" in it.
5 If a factory belonged to you, do you think you would be able to make a lot of money?
6 If you were a doctor, would you be able to help people who were ill?

7 Is Napoleon alive?

8 What happened to President Kennedy?

9 Is it usual for people in your country to eat hot food for breakfast?

10 What's the difference between "still" and "yet"?

11 When our shoes are dirty, what should we do?

12 Would you be afraid to go round the world in a small open boat?

13 What's the best way to guard against becoming ill?

14 What's the best way to calm somebody down when he's very angry?

15 If you were a millionaire, where would you live?

16 If you were a king, what would your wife be called?

17 When do we say "if I were you, ..."?

18 If you won a million pounds, what would you do with it?

19 What do we do with useless things?

20 Do you think that what you're learning now will be useful to you later on in life?

**Answers**

1 Yes, I think the lives of the poor are happier than those of the rich. ~ No, I don't think the lives of the poor are happier than those of the rich. I think they're less happy.

2 Yes, although I'm now able to hold a simple conversation in English, I think I should keep studying.

3 Yes, my mum cooks tasty food. ~ No, my mum doesn't cook tasty food.

4 I like reading all kinds of books, such as history books, science books etc.

5 Yes, if a factory belonged to me, I think I would be able to make a lot of money.

6 Yes, if I were a doctor, I could help people who were ill.

7 No, Napoleon isn't alive; he's dead.

8 President Kennedy was assassinated (in 1963).

9 Yes, it's usual for people in my country to eat hot food for breakfast. ~ No, it isn't usual for people in my country to eat hot food for breakfast.

10 The difference between "still" and "yet" is that we use "still" for something that is in progress at the moment, whereas we use "yet" for something that has not begun or happened. We generally use "still" in positive sentences, whereas we generally use "yet" in questions and negative sentences.

11 When our shoes are dirty, we should clean them.

12 Yes, I would be afraid to go round the world in a small open boat. ~ No, I wouldn't be afraid to go round the world in a small open boat.

13 The best way to guard against becoming ill is to eat healthy food, sleep well and do exercise.

14 The best way to calm somebody down when he's very angry is to speak quietly and pleasantly to him.

15 If I were a millionaire, I would live in ...

16 If I were a king, my wife would be called a queen.

17 We say "If I were you, ...", when we want to give advice to somebody, especially when we think perhaps there is a problem.

18 If I won ..., I would ...

19 We throw useless things away.

20 Yes, I think that what I'm learning now will be useful to me later on in life.

## Revision Exercise 30 (Lessons 64 - 65)

1 If a plant had no water, would it die?

2 If today were Sunday, what'd tomorrow be?

3 What kind of things do we put in sandwiches?

4 Are your dictations usually faultless?

5 What must two people or things have if we want to make a comparison between them?

6 Give me a sentence with "even" in it.

7 If you mixed some red and white paint together, what would you get?

8 Do you take good care of your health?

9 Would you take your time going home if somebody told you your house was on fire?

10 Do people hurry when they have plenty of time?

11 What's the difference between "for" and "since"?

12 Why do people use microwaves instead of normal cookers?

13 Do you hope your English studies will help your future career?

14 If you lent something to somebody and they didn't return it, what'd you do?

15 What's a film star?

16 What's the most agricultural region of your country?

17 If you keep somebody waiting for a long time, should you apologise?

18 How can we help to avoid becoming ill?

19 Do you like the fashion in clothes at the moment?

20 Why should you not worry if you don't immediately understand some of the grammar in this book?

**Answers**

1 Yes, if a plant had no water, it would die.

2 If today were Sunday, tomorrow'd be Monday.

3 We put meat, cheese, egg etc. in sandwiches.

4 No, my dictations aren't usually faultless; they usually contain mistakes.

5 If we want to make a comparison between two people or things, they must have something in common.

6 She speaks Russian, German, French, and even Chinese. ~

7 If I mixed some red and white paint together, I'd get pink paint.

8 Yes, I take good care of my health ~ No, I don't take good care of my health.

9 No, I wouldn't take my time going home if somebody told me my house was on fire; I'd hurry.

10 No, people don't hurry when they have plenty of time; they take their time.

11 The difference between "for" and "since" is that we use the word "for" when we say a period of time, whereas we use the word "since" when we say the point at which the period began.

12 People use microwaves instead of normal cookers because microwaves cook food more quickly than normal cookers.

13 Yes, I hope my English studies will help my future career.

14 If I lent something to somebody and they didn't return it, I'd ...

15 A film star is a famous actor or actress in the cinema world.

16 ... is the most agricultural region of my country.

17 Yes, if you keep somebody waiting for a long time, you should apologise.

18 We can help to avoid becoming ill by living a healthy life.

19 Yes, I like the fashion in clothes at the moment. ~ No, I don't like the fashion in clothes at the moment.

20 I shouldn't worry if I don't immediately understand some of the grammar in this book because I will practise it again in other lessons, and I can study it at home.

## Revision Exercise 31 (Lessons 66 – 67)

1 What were you doing at this time last Sunday?

2 About how much does a doctor earn a year in your country?

3 What does a man wear when he goes to a formal dinner?

4 How often do you go to the hairdresser's?

5 Why do you think some films are so popular?

6 What does a bathroom usually contain?

7 What does a mirror do?

8 How do we form the passive voice?

9 Now I am going to give you a sentence in the active voice, and I want you to put it into the passive voice: John ate the pasta.

10 Now I am going to give you a sentence in the active voice, and I want you to put it into the passive voice: My boss is going to write that email.

11 When you were a child, did your parents make you eat your vegetables?

12 Which would you prefer as a snack during a morning break: a bag of crisps or some biscuits?

13 How soon after you were born did you learn to walk?

14 What do we call the part of a tree that's in the land?

15 If you wanted to go from here to Scotland, would you have to cross the sea or would you be able to go all the way by land?

16 Is it safe for young children to cross the road on their own?

17 How long did you lie in bed for last night?

18 When do people use the words "sir" and "madam"?

19 When do we use the words "gentleman" and "lady"?

20 What's the standard height for a man (or woman) in your country?

**Answers**

1 I was ... at this time last Sunday.

2 A doctor earns about ... a year in my country.

3 A man wears a suit and tie when he goes to a formal dinner.

4 I go to the hairdresser's ... times a year.

5 I think some films are so popular because they tell interesting or exciting stories.

6 A bathroom usually contains a toilet, a basin, and a bath or shower.

7 A mirror reflects light.

8 We form the passive voice with the verb "to be" and a past participle.

9 The pasta was eaten by John.

10 That email is going to be written by my boss.

11 Yes, when I was a child, my parents made me eat my vegetables. ~ No, when I was a child, my parents didn't make me eat my vegetables.

12 I'd prefer ... as a snack during a morning break.

13 I learnt to walk about a year after I was born.

14 We call the part of a tree that's in the land the roots.

15 If I wanted to go from here to Scotland, I'd ...

16 No, it isn't safe for young children to cross the road on their own.

17 I lay in bed for ... hours last night.

18 People use the words "sir" and "madam" to be polite when they speak to customers.

19 We use the words "gentleman" and "lady" instead of "man" and "woman" when we want to sound polite.

20 The standard height for a man/woman in my country is ...

# Index

## Notes

## *Notes*

## Notes

# Notes

# Notes